NEW

CUTTING EDGE

ELEMENTARY

WORKBOOK

peter moor   sarah cunningham   frances eales

Longman

CONTENTS

Common words

1 **a** Rearrange the mixed-up letters to make common words.

1   n a m   man
2   m a w o n   _woman_
3   r e c h a t e _teacher_
4   h i r a c   _chair_
5   o r o d   _door_
6   y o b   _boy_
7   e k d s   _desk_
8   b o t e n o k o _notebook_
9   w o d w i n   _window_
10 d u n s e t t _student_
11 n e p   _pen_
12 l i r g   _girl_

b Look at page 6 of the Students' Book and check.

Numbers 0–21

2 Write the numbers.

a **1**
   one

b **4**
   four

c **15**
   fifteen

d **2**
   two

e **8**
   eight

f **20**
   twenty

g **3**
   three

h **12**
   twelve

Days of the week

3 **a** Write the missing letters to make the days of the week.

1	M o n d a y
2	T u e s d a y
3	W c d n e s d a y
4	Th r u e d a y
5	F r i d a y
6	S a t u r d a y
7	S u n d a y

b **T0.1** Listen and check your spelling.

Numbers 1–100

4 Do the calculation. Then write the numbers in full.

a **21 + 42 =** __63__

   twenty-one and forty-two is sixty-three

b **35 + 54 =** _89_

c **29 + 71 =** _100_

d **83 + 14 =** _97_

Names and countries

1 **a** Complete the conversation with the words in the box.

| My | this | your | Hello | you | name | 's | Nice |
| And | What |

SEBASTIAN: Hello. (1) _____My_____ name
(2) _____ Sebastian.
(3) _____'s (4) _____ name?

FLORENCE: My (5) _____'s Florence.

SEBASTIAN: (6) _____ to meet (7) _____ ,
Florence.

FLORENCE: (8) _____ you.

SEBASTIAN: And (9) _____ is my friend,
Charlotte.

FLORENCE: Hello, Charlotte.

CHARLOTTE: (10) _____ .

b **T1.1** Listen and repeat the conversation.

Personal information: *be*

2 Write the questions and answers.

a Ronaldo – Brazil
1 What 's his name?
2 His name's Ronaldo.
3 Where 's he from?
4 He 's from Brazil.

b Nicole Kidman – Australia

1 What ___her_____
_____name_____ ?
2 Her ___name's___
___Nicole Kidman.___
3 Where __is they___
___from___ ?
4 She __is from___
__A_____

c David and Victoria Beckham – England
1 What ___are their names___ ?
2 Their ___are David and Victoria Beckham.___
3 Where ___are they from___ ?
4 They ___are from England.___

d Jackie Chan – China
1 What _____
_____ ?
2 His ___name's____
_____
3 Where _____
_____ ?
4 He __is from__
__china.__

Nationalities

3 Find twelve nationalities in the word square.

```
A U S T R A L I A N
M E J T U R K I S H
E N A R S P A T P A
R U P O S I T K A B
I T A L I A N O N R
C A N I A N K R I I
A M E R N I M E S T
N O S W A T U A H I
F R E N C H A N O S
K O R I P O L I S H
A T U C H I N E S E
```

Vocabulary booster
More countries and nationalities

4 **a** Write the nationalities.

1	Thailand	Thai
2	Brazil	Brazilian
3	Switzerland	swiss
4	Hungary	
5	Mexico	
6	Canada	
7	Egypt	
8	Indonesia	
9	Ireland	
10	Argentina	

b **T1.2** Listen and check. Practise saying the countries and nationalities.

is or *are*

5 Complete the sentences with *is* or *are*.

a My name ___is___ Martina.

b Where ___are___ you from?

c ___is___ Walter from Germany?

d He _____ twenty-two years old.

e _____ Ross and Jennifer married?

f _____ you on holiday?

g Fernanda _____ a Spanish teacher.

Negative sentences

6 Make the sentences negative.

a Edinburgh is in England. *isn't*

b I'm from Ireland. *not*

c My mother and father are English. *aren't*

d Brazil is a small country. *isn't*

e My name is Lana. *isn't*

f My sister is married. *isn't*

g I'm fifteen years old.

h Philip and Elizabeth are on holiday.

Short answers

7 Write the short answers for the questions.

a Are you Portuguese?
  No, ___I'm not___ . I'm Brazilian.

b Is James English?
  Yes, _____ . He's from Manchester.

c Is your address 16 New Street?
  No, _____ . It's 26 New Road.

d Are you and your friend here on holiday?
  No, _____ . We're here on business.

e Is Barbara married?
  Yes, _____ . Her husband's a doctor.

f Are you married?
  Yes, _____ . This is my husband, James.

g Is Thomas an actor?
  No, _____ . He's a musician.

h Are Anne and Michael English?
  No, _____ . They're from Ireland.

i Is 'Howard' your surname?
  Yes, _____ . My first name's Tony.

j Is Jacqueline a teacher?
  No, _____ . She's a student.

Possessive adjectives

8 Look at the pictures and complete the sentences with *my*, *your*, *his*, *her*, *our* or *their*.

Hi! (a) ___My___ name's Ed Turner!
And this is (b) ___my___ wife.
(c) ___her___ name's Thelma. This is
(d) ___our___ house!!

This is Thelma with (e) ___our___ two
children – (f) ___their___ names are Bob
and Tracey – and (g) ___her___ brother
– (h) ___his___ name's Louis.

And this is (i) ___our___ dog. What's
(j) ___Your___ name, friend?

(k) ___my___ name's Bones.

Indefinite article: *a(n)*

9 Write *a* or *an*.

a ___an___ actor
b _____ businesswoman
c _____ e-mail address
d _____ lesson
e _____ telephone number
f _____ holiday
g _____ teacher
h _____ English teacher

Vocabulary
Jobs

10 Rearrange the mixed-up letters to make words for jobs. The first letter is underlined.

a r<u>a</u>c t o   _____actor_____
b s u r e <u>n</u>   _____
c e c l i p o   c<u>o</u>i f f e r   _____
d g r e n i <u>s</u>   _____
e p o <u>s</u> h   s t i t <u>a</u> n s s a   _____
f a n u <u>m</u> i s i c   _____
g r a w y e <u>l</u>   _____
h c l <u>e</u> r i t i n e a c   _____

be: personal questions

11 **a** Complete the questions with the words in the box.

| business   married   job   <u>name</u>   address |
| number   you   from |

1 What's your _____name_____ ?
2 Where are you _____ ?
3 Are you here on _____ ?
4 How old are ___you___ ?
5 What's your telephone ___number___ ?
6 Are you ___married___ ?
7 What's your e-mail _____ ?
8 What's your ___job___ ?

b **T1.3** Listen to the questions. Practise saying them.

Listen and read

12 **T1.4** Listen to and/or read about four people from different places. Who:

a is an actress? _____Béatrice Santini_____

b is a taxi driver? _____Donna Fiorelli_____

c is from France? _____Beatrice santine_____

d are musicians? _____Plankton_____

e is from London? _____David mills_____

f is from Edinburgh? _____Betty Booth_____

g is a bus driver? _____David mills_____

h is 45 years old? _____Donna Fiorelli_____

People from different places

Béatrice Santini

Béatrice Santini is from France. She's 28 years old, and she's an actress. She's married; her husband is film director, Karol Bolewski. Karol is 56 years old. Their home is in Paris.

Donna Fiorelli

Donna Fiorelli is from New York. She's a taxi driver. She's 45 years old. Is she married? 'Yes, I am . . . I'm married to my job.'

David Mills

'Hello. My name is David Mills. I'm 37 years old, and I'm single. I'm a bus driver in London. I'm also a writer: my first book is *Bus Driver on Holiday*.'

Plankton

Allan, Doug, Richard and Kirsty are Plankton . . . four musicians from Aberdeen, in Scotland. Their manager is Betty Booth. Betty is from Edinburgh, and she's 25 years old.

Punctuation: capital letters

LOOK!

We use capital letters for:

– names	*Lara Croft*
– titles	*Mr Brown, Doctor Todd*
– countries	*China*
– nationalities	*Brazilian*
– roads	*Fifth Avenue*
– towns/cities	*Istanbul*
– the beginning of sentences	*What's your name?*

13 Circle the capital letters.

a she's mrs sarah grant.

b my mother's from the united states.

c are you spanish?

d our school is in camden road.

e i'm from rome.

f eric lives in berlin.

Improve your writing
Addresses in English

14 **a** Look at the address on this envelope.

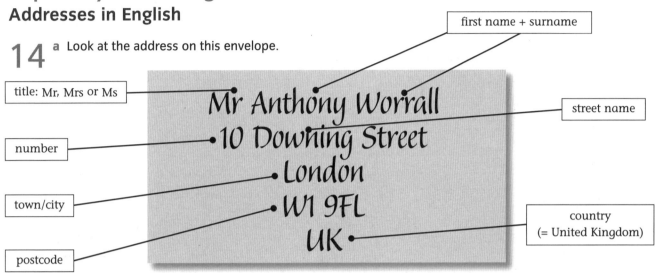

title: Mr, Mrs or Ms

first name + surname

street name

number

town/city

postcode

Mr Anthony Worrall
10 Downing Street
London
W1 9FL
UK

country
(= United Kingdom)

b Write these addresses in the correct order.

1 SW15 6GS – South London College – UK – London –
Richmond Road – 52

~~52~~ South London college
52 Richmond Road
~~~~London
SW15 6GS
UK

2 Dublin – 4 – Ireland – Mary Burke – Mrs –
109 St Stephen Street

Mrs Mary Burke
109 St stephen
Dubline
4
Irland

c Write the capital letters.

miss sarah ellis	Miss Sarah Ellis
62 high street	62 High street
amersham	Amersham
hp7 6dj	HP 7 6 DJ
england	England
mr simon henderson	Mr Simon Henderson
12 muirfield road	12 Muirfied Road
glasgow	Glasgow
g12 8sj	G 12 8 SJ
scotland	Scotland

Pronunciation
/ɒ/, /eɪ/ **and** /aɪ/

15 **a** **T1.5** Listen to the pronunciation of
these words. Practise saying them.

/ɒ/	/eɪ/	/aɪ/
what	name	I
from	age	fine
holiday	they	my

b **T1.6** Listen to the words. Write /ɒ/, /eɪ/
or /aɪ/.

1 write _____/aɪ/_____
2 eight _____
3 job _____
4 doctor _____
5 nine _____
6 Spain _____
7 nice _____
8 not _____

Identifying objects: *this*, *that*, *these*, *those*

1 Describe the pictures, using *this*, *that*, *these* or *those*.

a _____this_____ car

b __this__ shoes

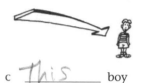

c __This__ boy

d __This__ coat

e __This__ chairs

f __This__ men

a/an or *no article* with objects and plurals

2 What's in the bag? Write *a*, *an* or – (*no article*).

a _____a_____ mobile phone
b ____an____ English dictionary
c _____a_____ camera
d _____ address book
e _____ keys
f _____a_____ photos
g _____ diary
h _____ identity card

have/has got

3 a Read the information in the table. Complete the sentences with *'s got, hasn't got, 've got* or *haven't got*.

	Silvia	Martin and Inge	Alfonso
Pet?	dog (Rex)	no	two cats
Car?	yes – an Audi	two	no
Computer?	no	yes	yes

1 Silvia ___'s got___ a dog – his name's Rex.
2 She ___has___ a car – it's an Audi.
3 She ___has___ a computer.
4 Martin and Inge ___got___ a pet.
5 They ___have___ two cars.
6 They ___have___ a computer.
7 Alfonso _____ two cats.
8 He _____ a car.
9 He _____ a computer.

b **T2.1** Listen and check. Practise saying the sentences.

Questions and short answers

> **Have** I/you/we/they **got** | a dog?
> a car?
>
> **Yes**, I/you/we **have**.
> **No**, I/you/we **haven't**.
>
> **Has** he/she/it **got** | a computer?
> **Yes**, he/she/it **has**.
> **No**, he/she/it **hasn't**.

4 **a** Look back at the information about Silvia, Martin and Inge, and Alfonso. Complete the questions and answers below.

1 ___Has___ Silvia ___got___ a dog?

 ___Yes, she has.___

2 _____ she _____ a car?

 _____

3 _____ she _____ a computer?

 _____

4 _____ Martin and Inge _____ a pet?

 _____

5 _____ they _____ a car?

 _____

6 _____ they _____ a computer?

 _____

7 _____ Alfonso _____ a pet?

 _____

8 _____ he _____ a car?

 _____

9 _____ he _____ a computer?

 _____

b **T2.2** Listen and check your answers. Practise saying the questions and short answers.

's = is or has

5 **a** In the paragraph below, 's is missing nine times. Write 's in the correct places.

> My friend Steve's got a fantastic life. He only 21, but he got a great job – he a professional footballer – and he got lots of money. He got a new car, too – it a Porsche. It white and it got everything, even a CD player!

b Does 's = is or has?

1	___has___	4	_____	7	_____
2	_____	5	_____	8	_____
3	_____	6	_____	9	_____

Adjectives and nouns

> **Adjectives:**
>
> – go **before** nouns   *a comfortable car*
> – do **not** change   *blue eyes*
> – do **not** use *and*   *a large red hat*

6 Put the adjective in the correct place in the sentences.

a Max has got a car – it's a BMW. (German)
 Max has got a German car — it's a BMW.

b Your dog has got eyes. (beautiful)

 _____

c We've got two cats at home. (black)

 _____

d I've got a computer game – Crash 5!!! (fantastic)

 _____

e My friend Al is a musician. (professional)

 _____

f Lauren Bacall is my actress. (favourite)

 _____

g My sister's got a mobile phone. (new)

 _____

h Goldie is a dog. (friendly)

 _____

Vocabulary booster
More everyday objects

7 **a** Match the objects with the words in the box.

a passport	6	a mirror	5
a lipstick	4	a lighter	3
a driving licence	2	a comb	1
an alarm clock	8	painkillers	10
a toothbrush	7	sun screen	11
an MP3 player	9	toothpaste	12

b T2.3 Listen and check. Practise saying the words.

Vocabulary
Family vocabulary

8 **a** Look at the picture and information about the Doyle family. Use the information to complete the sentences.

1 Joe is Brenda's ___husband___ .
2 Jason is Joe's ___son___ .
3 Brenda is Jason's ___mother___ .
4 Joe is Jane's ___father___ .
5 Joe and Brenda are Jane's ___parents___ .
6 Colin is Jane's ___husband___ .
7 Jason is Sam's ___brother___ .
8 Jane is Sam's ___daughter___ .

b Answer the questions with two sentences, as in the example.

1 Who is Nora Walker?
   She's Brenda and Sam's mother. She's Jane and Jason's grandmother.

2 Who is Jason?
   _____

3 Who is Sam?
   _____

4 Who is Brenda?
   _____

5 Who is Jane?
   _____

6 Who are Jane and Jason?
   _____

Sam Doyle – Brenda's brother

Brenda Doyle – Joe's wife

Colin Best – Jane's husband

Joe Doyle – 'Dad'

Jason Doyle – Jane's brother

Jane Best – Joe and Brenda's daughter

Nora Walker (Nana) – Brenda's mother

Listen and read

9 a [T2.4] Listen to and/or read the text about the Iglesias family.

A famous family

Julio Iglesias is from Spain. The world's number 1 Spanish singer in the 70s and 80s, with songs like *Begin the Beguine*, he is now the father of a famous family. The three children from his marriage in the 1970s to actress Isabel Preysler – two sons and a daughter – are now all famous too.

His daughter, Chabeli, is a journalist in Washington, in the United States. His sons' names are Julio Junior and Enrique: Julio Junior is a model, actor and singer. His songs are in English and Spanish.

Enrique Iglesias is also a famous singer. His home is in Miami, Florida. He's got two Porsche cars at home!!

b Complete the information in the family tree about the Iglesias family.

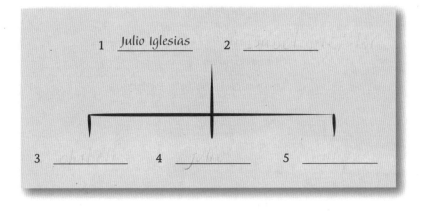

1 Julio Iglesias 2 _____

3 _____ 4 _____ 5 _____

c Put the questions in the correct order.

1 Iglesias – Where – is – Julio – from?

  Where is Julio Iglesias from?

2 children's – are – What – his – names?

  _____ ?

3 they – Are – all – famous?

  _____ ?

4 Isabel – is – Preysler – Who?

  _____ ?

5 job – Chabeli's – is – What?

  _____ ?

6 Junior – Julio – singer – Is – a?

  _____ ?

7 Enrique's – Where – home – is?

  _____ ?

8 Porsche – got – Has – a – Enrique?

  _____ ?

d Answer the questions 1–8 above.

1 He's from Spain.

2 His singer spanish.

3 _____

4 _____

5 _____

6 _____

7 _____

8 _____

Possessive 's

10 Write 's in the correct place in the sentences, as in the example.

a Patrick is Jane's brother.

b Is that Michael car?

c It's Tessa birthday on Saturday.

d What's your mother name?

e Where's Philip desk?

f My husband name is Peter.

g Jo is my sister friend.

h Carla house is in the centre of Rome.

Spelling
Plurals

11 a Write the plural of the words.

1 diary   _diaries_

2 dictionary

3 box

4 university

5 baby

6 key

7 match

8 watch   _watches_

9 house

10 bus   _buses_

11 address

12 boy   _boys_

b What are these irregular plurals?

1 child   _children_

2 woman

3 businessman

4 wife

5 life

6 person

Pronunciation
The sounds /s/ and /z/

12 a **T2.5** Listen to the pronunciation of the /s/ sound. Underline the /s/ sounds.

– What's this?
– It's my passport.

b **T2.6** Listen to the pronunciation of the /z/ sound. Circle the /z/ sounds.

His friend's name is James.

c **T2.7** Listen. Underline the /s/ sounds.

1 This is my sister. Her name's Suzanne.

2 Those are my keys!

3 She's seven years old.

4 What's his address?

5 She's got fantastic blue eyes.

6 What's your brother's first name?

7 Sarah is a famous actress.

8 What's the answer to this question?

d Listen again. Circle the /z/ sounds.

Prepositions

13 Choose the correct preposition.

a What's that at / in English?

b Have you got your diary for / with you?

c We've got two dogs at / in our family.

d John is a student at / for Cambridge University.

e We've got cable TV at / to home.

f I've got a pen in / on my bag.

g Chris is here on / for holiday.

h This watch is to / from Switzerland.

Question words

14 Complete the questions with the words in the box.

~~Who~~	How	~~Where~~	~~What~~	How
What	~~How~~	~~What~~	Who	What

a   *What*   's your surname ?

b   How   do you spell it?

c   Who   's that man over there?

d   What   colour is your car?

e   How   old is your nephew?

f   does 'niece' mean?

g   Where   is your father from?

h   Who   's your favourite actor?

i   How   do you say this word?

j   What   have you got in your bag?

Improve your writing
Combining sentences

15 Make one sentence using *and* and pronouns.

a My sister's married. My sister's got two children.
My sister's married and she's got two children.

b My father's 42. My father's a lawyer.
My Father 42 and his a lawyer

c My cousin Steve is 33. Steve isn't married.
My cousin steve is 33. He isn't maried

d My parents have got a new car. The new car is fantastic!
My Parents have got a new car.

e Prague is the capital of the Czech Republic. Prague is very beautiful.

f Maria and I are on holiday. Maria and I are in Thailand now.

Writing about your family

16 a Read about the people in this family.

People in my family

My father's name is Martin Hancock. He's fifty-three years old and he's an architect. He and my mother aren't married now – they're divorced. His new wife's name is Judy. They've got a baby daughter – her name's Cassandra and she's beautiful!!!

My sister, Caroline, is twenty-eight years old, and she's a teacher. She's married. Her husband's name is Marcos – he's from Chile. They've got two daughters: Rebecca, who's five, and Annabel, who's two years old. I'm their aunt!!

My cousin Martha is from Australia. She's nineteen years old, and she isn't married: she's a student at the University of Melbourne. She's got a boyfriend – his name is Mark. He's twenty. He isn't a student: he's a professional musician. The name of his group is MC2.

My grandmother is about eighty years old. Her name is Beatrice. She's got six children – four sons and two daughters – and she's got twenty-three grandchildren!!

b Write sentences about some people in your family.

Examples:
My father's name is Karl.
My sister, Mirjana, is twenty years old.

MODULE 3

Vocabulary
Common verbs

1 Match three words or phrases from the box to each verb below.

meat	in a ~~small~~ house	~~Spanish~~
coffee	to work	with my family
for Nike	economics	~~French~~
law	long hours	a lot of fish
water	mineral	~~Japanese~~
to university	black tea	to the cinema a lot
in Mexico City	in an office	in restaurants a lot
at university		

a speak _Spanish, French, Japanese_

b live _small house and family_

c work _coffee_

d go _cinema_

e study _to university_

f eat _meat_

g drink _water_

Present simple
Questions

2 a Complete the questions with a word.

1 Do you ___live___ in Edinburgh?

2 _____ your parents speak English?

3 Do you and your brother go _o wsd_ a lot?

4 Do you _like_ green tea?

5 Do you and your family live _In_ a flat?

6 Do Ben and James _goes_ German?

7 Do you eat a lot _____ chocolate?

8 Do all the students _____ law?

9 Do you _____ with your parents?

10 Do you work _____ hours?

b `T3.1` Listen and check. Practise saying the questions.

Negatives

3 a Join a sentence beginning with an ending to make negative sentences.

1 Most people don't work — economics.

2 Maoris don't come from — at the weekend.

3 People in Brazil don't speak — Australia.

4 Babies don't go — meat.

5 Most children don't study — to school.

6 Vegetarians don't eat — Spanish.

b `T3.2` Listen and check. Practise saying the sentences.

Positive and negative

4 a Read the information about Thomas and Angela, from Sweden, and Julia and Ken, from Singapore.

Thomas and Angela

home	a five-bedroom house in a small town in Sweden
languages	Swedish, English, German
jobs	they're lawyers
hobbies	the cinema
drinks	mineral water and coffee
food	Swedish and Italian food

Julia and Ken

home	a small flat in the centre of Singapore city
languages	English, Chinese, Malay
jobs	they're teachers
hobbies	eating in restaurants
drinks	tea
food	Chinese food

b Complete the sentences.

1 Thomas and Angela ___don't live___ in a big city.
2 They _____ in a big house.
3 They _____ English.
4 They _____ Chinese.
5 They _____ in a school.
6 They _____ to the cinema a lot.
7 They _____ mineral water.
8 They _____ Chinese food.
9 Julia and Ken ___live___ in a big city.
10 They _live_ in a big house.
11 They _speaks_ Chinese and English.
12 They _____ in an office.
13 They _____ in a school.
14 They _____ to the cinema a lot.
15 They _____ coffee.
16 They _____ Chinese food.

Questions and short answers

5 Answer the questions about Thomas and Angela, and Julia and Ken with short answers. Then answer the questions about yourself.

a Do Thomas and Angela live in a small town?
Yes, they do.

Do you live in a small town? _No, I don't._

b Do they work in an office? _____

Do you work in an office? _____

c Do they speak Chinese? _No, They don't_
Do you speak Chinese? _Yes, I do_

d Do they drink tea? _No, They don't_
Do you drink tea? _Yes, I do_

e Do Julia and Ken live in a big city? _____

Do you live in a big city? _____

f Do they go to the cinema a lot? _Yes, They do_

Do you go to the cinema a lot? _No, I don't_

g Do they eat Italian food? _Yes, They do_

Do you eat Italian food? _No, I don't_

h Do they drink tea? _____

Do you drink tea? _____

Vocabulary booster
Buildings

6 **a** Label the buildings with words in the box.

| a block of flats   a library   a school   a bank |
| a supermarket   a railway station   a hospital   a hotel |

1 _a block of flats_   2 _a school_

3 _a hospital_   4 _a library_

5 _a hotel_   6 _a supermarket_

7 _a railway station_   8 _a bank_

b **T3.3** Listen and check. Practise saying the words.

Listen and read

7 a **T3.4** Listen to and/or read the text about young people in South Korea.

Studying in South Korea

What time do you have breakfast?
Where do you have lunch?
Do you go out with your friends for a coffee after school or after work?
Do you work in the evenings, or do you have dinner with family or friends?

Life is very different for many young people in South Korea. It's very important for people to go to a good university, and find a good job . . . so study is very, very important! Young people get up at about six o'clock, have breakfast with their family, and then go to school . . . schools in South Korea start at seven o'clock.

After five hours of lessons in the morning, it's time for lunch. Most people have lunch at school. Then there are more lessons until six o'clock . . . but that's not the end! Many young Koreans go to the library and study from about eight o'clock to eleven or twelve o'clock, when the libraries close.

At that time, they go home in a special minibus. Most students don't go to bed before one or two o'clock, and then the next day, after just four or five hours of sleep, it's time to get up again!

b Answer the questions.

1 What time do most young people get up in South Korea?

   They get up at about six o'clock.

2 What time do schools start in South Korea?

   They start school seven o'clock

3 Where do most young people have lunch?

4 What time do schools in South Korea finish?

   at twelve

5 Where do many young people go in the evening?

6 What time do the libraries close?

   at twelve

7 How do students go home?

   no they stay living 2 or twelveo'clock

8 What time do they go to bed?

   Five hours

Vocabulary
Opposites

8 Rearrange the letters to make opposites. Look at page 28 of the Students' Book, if necessary.

a finish   a r t s t

   start

b morning   v i n e n e g

   Evening

c go to bed   t e g p u

   Jet up

d open   s o l c e

   Close

e go out   m o c e m e h o

f a snack   a g i b l a m e

g start school v a l e e l o s c o h

h the week   h e t n e w d e k e

Telling the time

9 Write the times.

a _It's ten past eight._

b _____

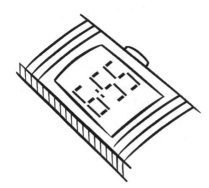

c _____

d _____

e _____

f _____

g _____

h _____

i _____

Prepositions of time: *in*, *at* or *to*

10 Complete the sentences with *in*, *at* or *to*.

a It's seven o'clock __in__ the morning.

b Do you have a big lunch _on_ Sunday?

c I get up _at_ six o'clock.

d We work from eight to twelve _in_ the morning.

e Shops don't stay open _at_ night.

f I finish work at seven o'clock _in_ the evening.

g Do you go out a lot _____ the weekend?

h The children don't sleep _____ the afternoon.

Vocabulary
Daily routines

11 Match the verbs with the nouns.

a have   the bus
b read   home
c go to   lunch
d have   bed late
e have a   the newspaper
f watch   shower
g come   dinner
h catch   work
i go to   TV

Subject and object pronouns

> *LOOK!*
>
> *I, you, he, she, it, we* and *they* are **subject pronouns**.
>
> *me, you, him, her, it, us* and *them* are **object pronouns**.
>
> | subject pronoun | | object pronoun |
> |---|---|---|
> | I | ⇨ | me |
> | you | ⇨ | you |
> | he | ⇨ | him |
> | she | ⇨ | her |
> | it | ⇨ | it |
> | we | ⇨ | us |
> | they | ⇨ | them |
>
> We use object pronouns:
>
> • after prepositions.
>   *Come with* **me**.
>
> • when the pronoun is the object of the sentence.
>   *Sarah knows* **him**.

12 Correct the pronouns in bold, as in the example.

a A: What's her name?

   B: Karen.

   A: How do you spell ~~her~~? *it*

b Is that letter for **I**?

c A: What time is your bus?

   B: I catch **her** at half past seven.

d A: Is that your brother?

   B: Yes, it is, but who's that with **he**?

e A: My favourite TV programme is *ER*. Do you watch **them**?

   B: No, I don't.

f A: What's Sally's address?

   B: I don't know. I haven't got **him** with **I**.

g We've got a big flat and my grandparents live with **we**.

h A: Who are those people?

   B: I don't know **they**.

Pronunciation
The letter *i*

13 a **T3.5** We pronounce the letter *i* in different ways. Listen to these examples.

/ɪ/ live, city   /aɪ/ I, like

b Look at the words in the box. Do we pronounce *i* as /ɪ/ or as /aɪ/? Put the words into the correct column.

drink six big ~~life~~ finish this time nine
five children ~~write~~ listen night dinner

/ɪ/		/aɪ/	
drink		life	
write			
finished			

c **T3.6** Listen and check. Practise saying the words.

Improve your writing
Commas, full stops, *and* and *but*

> *LOOK!*
>
> | , | a comma |
> | . | a full stop |
> | linkers | *and, but* |

14 a Write a comma, a full stop and a linker in the sentence below.

In Britain children start school at about 9 o'clock in the morning in Poland they start school at 8 o'clock

b Use the information in the box to write sentences about the differences between life in New York and life in York, a town in the north of England. Use commas, full stops, *and* or *but*.

	New York, USA	York, UK
Most people live in	flats (= apartments)	houses
Most people start work	8 am	9 am
Most people finish work	6 pm	5.30 pm
Children start school at	5 years	4 years
Most shops open at	9 am	9 am
Most shops close at	8 pm	6 pm

York

New York

too, *both* and *neither*

We use *me too* to agree with a positive sentence.

A: **I've got a cat.**
B: *Me too!!*

We use *me neither* to agree with a negative sentence.

A: *I'm not married.*
B: **Me neither.**

We use *both* to say that two things or people are the same. Notice the position of *both*.

*We **both** like jazz.*
*They are **both** ten years old.*

1 (New York / live / York /live)
   In New York most people live in apartments, but in York most people
   live in houses.

2 (New York / start work / finish work)
   In New York most people start work at 8 am, and they finish work
   at 6 pm.

3 (New York / start work / York)

4 (York / start work / finish work)

5 (New York / finish work / York)

6 (New York / children start school / York)

7 (New York / shops open / close)

8 (New York / shops close / York)

15 Complete the sentences *both*, *neither* or *too*.

a A: Are you from the USA?
   B: Yes, I'm from California.
   A: Oh really? Me ___too___ !

b Paula and her sister are _____ teachers.

c A: We're here on holiday. How about you?
   B: Yes, me _____ .

d A: I don't understand this film.
   B: Me _____ .

e Nick and I _____ work at *The Bridge Hotel*.

f A: I don't take milk in my coffee.
   B: No, me _____ .

g A: I don't go to bed late.
   B: Me _____ .

h A: I read *The Economist*.
   B: Me _____ .

MODULE 4

Present simple
Spelling

1 Write the letters to make the *he/she/it* form.

a My mother read_s_ *Hi!* magazine.

b James watch_ _ TV in the morning.

c Winnie come_ from South Korea.

d Richard live_ in the United States.

e She go_ _ to bed at eleven o'clock.

f Francis enjoy_ watching football on TV.

g My brother say_ he's fine.

h Norma stud_ _ _ economics at the University of Leeds.

i Ian always play_ football on Saturday.

Present simple with *he/she/it*

2 a Look at the information in the chart and complete these sentences about Akiko Murata.

1 She _____comes_____ (come) from Japan.

2 She _____ (study) fashion design.

3 She _____ (live) in San Francisco.

4 She _____ (speak) Japanese and English.

5 She _____ (like) cooking and ballet.

b [T4.1] Listen and check. Practise saying the sentences.

	Nationality	Job	Address	Languages	Hobbies
Akiko Murata	Japanese	fashion design student	Golden Gate Ave. San Francisco, USA	Japanese, English	cooking, ballet
David Jones	British	English teacher	The English School, Seoul, South Korea	English, French, Korean	watching football, playing the guitar
Beatriz Ayala	Argentinian	bank employee	Carrer Bonavista Barcelona, Spain	Spanish, Catalan, English	painting, going to the gym
Zoltan Tarnai	Hungarian	music teacher	Rue d'Alleray, Paris, France	Hungarian, French, German	playing tennis, walking

c Write sentences about David, Beatriz and Zoltan using the Present simple.

1 David _teaches English._ (teach)

2 He _____ (come from)

3 _____ (live)

4 _____ (speak)

5 _____ (play)

6 Beatriz _lives in Spain._ (live)

7 She _____ (come from)

8 _____ (speak)

9 _____ (work)

10 _____ (go to the gym)

11 Zoltan _speaks Hungarian, French and German._ (speak)

12 He _____ (come from)

13 _____ (live)

14 _____ (teach)

15 _____ (play)

Short answers

3 **a** Look at the information about Akiko and David on page 22 and write the correct short answer.

1   Does Akiko come from Japan?   _Yes, she does._

2   Does she study economics?   _No, she doesn't._

3   Does she live in New York?   _____

4   Does she speak English?   _____

5   Does she like ballet?   _____

6   Does David come from the USA?   _____

7   Does he teach English?   _____

8   Does he live in South Korea?   _____

9   Does he speak Chinese?   _____

10   Does he play tennis?   _____

b **T4.2** Listen and check. Practise saying the questions and short answers.

Negatives

4 **a** Make these sentences negative.

1   Maria likes studying grammar.

    Maria doesn't like studying grammar.

2   It rains in summer.

    _____

3   My brother likes getting up at seven o'clock.

    _____

4   The restaurant closes on Sunday evening.

    _____

5   Martin comes to class every week.

    _____

6   Tony buys all his food at the supermarket.

    _____

7   Carla drives to work.

    _____

8   My cousin visits me every month.

    _____

b **T4.3** Listen and check. Practise saying the sentences.

Positives and negatives

5 Put the verbs in brackets into the correct form of the Present simple.

Malcolm Tracey (a) _doesn't go_ (not go) to work: he only (b) _____ (leave) his home town to go on holiday in the Caribbean. But Malcolm is a millionaire. He (c) _____ (write) books about money, and how to make a lot of it. His new book is called _Easy Money: How to make money without getting out of bed._ Malcolm (d) _____ (live) in a large house near London. He (e) _____ (get up) at about eight o'clock in the morning, and (f) _____ (have) breakfast with his family. After breakfast, he (g) _____ (drive) his children to school, and (h) _____ (read) the newspaper in the garden until lunchtime. After lunch, he (i) _____ (buy) and (j) _____ (sell) on the Internet. He (k) _____ (finish) work at four o'clock when his children come home. 'I've got a simple system for making money,' Malcolm (l) _____ (say). 'It (m) _____ (not work) for everybody ... but it (n) _____ (work) for me!!'

Questions

6 Write questions about Malcolm.

a   (Where / live)   _Where does he live?_

b   (When / get up) _____

c   (What / do / after breakfast) _____

d   (Where / read the newspaper) _____

e   (Where / go on holiday) _____

f   (What / do after lunch) _____

Vocabulary booster
Everyday activities

7 **a** Match the phrases in the box with the pictures below.

clean your teeth ☐	have a shower ☐1	go for a walk ☐	catch a bus ☐	go to the gym ☐
get dressed ☐	wake up ☐	go for a run ☐	cook a meal ☐	meet friends ☐

b **T4.4** Listen and check. Practise saying the phrases.

like, love, hate + -ing

8 **a** Read about Irene and Agnes and find out what they like and dislike about their life.

> Irene and Agnes are both au pairs: they live with a family, do housework (clean the house) and help with the children. In the afternoon, they go to an English class. In the evenings, they often babysit.

1 = It's horrible!!! I hate it!   4 = I like it.
2 = I don't like it.   5 = It's fantastic!!! I love it!!
3 = OK

	Irene	Agnes
taking the children to school	2	4
doing housework	1	5
talking to the family	5	2
going to English class	4	1
babysitting	2	4

b Write about their likes and dislikes.

1 (taking the children to school)

   Irene doesn't like taking the children to school.

   Agnes likes taking the children to school.

2 (doing housework)

   Irene _____.

   Agnes _____.

3 (talking to the family)

   Irene _____.

   Agnes _____.

4 (going to English class)

   Irene _____.

   Agnes _____.

5 (babysitting)

   Irene _____.

   Agnes _____.

Listen and read

9 a `T4.5` Listen to and/or read to the text about English people's homes abroad.

An Englishman's home ...

'An Englishman's home', they say, 'is his castle.' Perhaps that's true ... but nowadays the home often isn't in England ... it's abroad!

More than half a million British people have a second home in another country. Many buy old houses in the south of France, or in Tuscany, in the north of Italy. The Eurostar train, which goes from London to Paris in three hours, makes it easy to go from one home to the other quickly.

The Noteman family, who live in London, have got a small house in Gascony. They sometimes go there for weekends, and they always spend the summer in France with their four children. Jerry Noteman says, 'We really like living in France: the weather is usually good, we like the food and the wine and the people are very friendly. We don't usually speak French when we go out ... most of our neighbours in the village are English, too!'

b Answer these questions.

1 How many British people have a home abroad?
   More than half a million.

2 Where do they often buy houses?
   _____

3 Where does the Eurostar train go to?
   _____

4 Where do the Noteman family live in England?
   _____

5 Where do they live in France?
   _____

6 Where do they spend the summer?
   _____

7 How many children do they have?
   _____

8 What do they like about living in France?
   _____

9 Where do most of their neighbours come from?
   _____

Pronouns

10 Replace the words in bold with a pronoun from the box.

him	~~it~~	she	them	it	her	they	it
them							

a Is your ice-cream OK? Do you like ~~your ice-cream~~? ___it___

b A: Do you like cats?

   B: Yes, I love **cats**. _____

c I love flying – I think **flying** is great. _____

d I've got twelve brothers and sisters and **my brothers and sisters** are all married. _____

e I don't like dogs – I'm frightened of **dogs**. _____

f Jon doesn't like me and I hate **Jon**! _____

g A: Do you enjoy flying?

   B: No, I hate **flying**. _____

h A: Do you like Diana?

   B: Yes, I love **Diana**! I think **Diana's** fantastic!

   _____ _____

Adverbs of frequency

11 Choose the correct alternative.

a In the morning, the sun *always* / *never* / *sometimes* comes up in the east.

b Sharks *never* / *sometimes* / *often* kill people.

c Children *never* / *don't often* / *usually* like sweets.

d In the game of chess, black *always* / *never* / *usually* starts.

e People with brown hair *don't often* / *never* / *often* have brown eyes.

f Monday *always* / *often* / *usually* comes before Tuesday.

g A year *always* / *never* / *usually* has 364 days.

h Spiders *always* / *often* / *sometimes* have eight legs.

Activity verbs

12 Complete the sentences with the verbs in the box.

read	write	watch	listen	plays	go	visit
study	write	read	go	listen		

a A: Do you ___read___ the newspaper every day?

   B: No, I don't. I only ___read___ magazines.

b A: Do you ever _____ swimming at the weekend?

   B: No, I don't, but I often _____ shopping!

c My mother and father always _____ a video on a Friday night.

d I usually _____ to a CD when I drive to work. I never _____ to the radio.

e My brother Hector loves sport: he _____ rugby, basketball, tennis and chess!!

f I never _____ letters, but I _____ a lot of e-mails!!

g I always _____ my friend Roger when I'm in London.

h A: I'm at Edinburgh University.

   B: What do you _____ ?

   A: Law.

Word order: frequency adverbs, auxiliaries

13 Put the words in brackets in the correct places in the sentences, as in the example.

a *sometimes*
   I have dinner at my friend's house. (sometimes)

b Caroline eats fish. (never)

c I often eat in a restaurant. (don't)

d I get up late on a Sunday morning. (usually)

e It's very hot in August in my city. (always)

f The Brown family usually to Italy on holiday. (go)

g The weather always cold in January. (is)

h The bus is late. (often)

Pronunciation
Plural nouns with /s/, /z/ and /ɪz/

14 a **T4.6** Listen and notice the pronunciation of the plural form of these words.

shop	shops	/s/
key	keys	/z/
bus	buses	/ɪz/

b Write the plural form of the nouns below. Do we pronounce the *s* at the end of the word as /s/, /z/ or /ɪz/?

1 dog_   ___/z/___
2 crowd_   _____
3 spider_   _____
4 actress_   _____
5 beach_   _____
6 driver_   _____
7 student_   _____
8 restaurant_   _____
9 house_   _____
10 friend_   _____
11 parent_   _____
12 address_   _____

c **T4.7** Listen to the pronunciation of the words. Practise saying them.

Asking politely

15 Put the words in the correct order.

a   want – Do – tea – you – a ?

  Do you want a tea?

b   like – Excuse – please – coffees – 'd – two – I – me

  _____

  _____

c   of – those – I – like – one – please – 'd

  _____

  _____

d   bill – like – 'd – me – Excuse – please – I – the

  _____

  _____

e   milk – you – with – want – your – Do – tea ?

  _____

  _____

Apostrophes

16 Add apostrophes to the sentences.

a   A: Anything else?

     B: No thanks, Im fine.

b   Id like a coffee but I dont want milk, thank you.

c   A: Whats the time?

     B: Im sorry, I havent got a watch.

d   A: Do you want a drink?

     B: Thats a good idea!

e   Is that Elenas bag?

Improve your writing
A paragraph about a friend

17 **a** Match the questions and answers.

1   What's his name?

2   Where does he come from?

3   Where does he live now?

4   What does he do?

5   Where does he play?

6   What does he like about life in London?

7   What does he dislike about life in London?

8   What does he think of the people?

a   He's a musician.

b   In a bar called *East and West*.

c   Takashi.

d   They're very nice when you know them.

e   The rain.

f   In London.

g   Okinawa, in Japan.

h   The international atmosphere.

b Use the information to write a paragraph about Takashi, like this:

My friend Takashi _____ Okinawa, in Japan, but now he _____ in London _____ a musician, and _____ in a bar called *East and West*. He _____ the international atmosphere in London, but _____ the rain! He _____ the people are very nice _____ .

Vocabulary

Means of transport

1 Write the missing letters.

a B U S

b M _ T _ R B _ K _

c S C _ _ T _ R

d B _ C _ CL _

e _ _ R _ PL _ N _

f T R _ M

g T R _ _ N

h _ N D _ R G R _ _ N D
or S _ B W _ Y

i T _ X _

Prepositions

2 Complete the sentences with *by, to, on, off, for* or *from*.

a   Most people go to work _____by_____ car.

b   It's not possible to drive to the beach: go ___on_____ foot.

c   My journey _____to_____ work takes about 30 minutes.

d   In Thailand, cars drive _____on_____ the left.

e   You can fly _____ Scotland direct from Paris.

f   This is where you wait _____ a bus to the railway station.

g   Please wait for people to get _____ the bus before you get _____ .

h   I never walk _____ town: I always go _____ bus.

i   This bus goes _____ the airport to the city centre.

can/can't

3 Look at the motorway signs. What can/can't you do on the motorway? Complete the sentences.

a   You _____*can't*_____ stop on the motorway.

b   You _____ drive at 100 kilometres an hour.

c   You _____ drive at 180 kilometres an hour.

d   You _____ ride a bicycle on the motorway.

e   You _____ walk on the motorway.

f   You _____ find something to eat and drink at the service station.

g   You _____ buy petrol at the service station.

h   You _____ turn round.

i   Learner drivers _____ use the motorway.

Short answers

> **Short answers with *can***
> **Can** I/you/he/she/we/they drive?
> Yes, I/you/he/she/we/they **can**.
> No, I/you/he/she/we/they **can't**.

4 **a** Write the short answers.

NO PARKING
MONDAY - SATURDAY 9.30 - 5.30

1 It's 8.30 in the morning. Can I park here? _Yes, you can._

2 Can I park here on a Sunday? _____

NO SMOKING

3 Can I smoke here? _____

SORRY No children under 18

4 Tom and Barbara are sixteen years old.
Can they go in? _____

5 I'm nineteen years old. Can I go in? _____

WALK

6 Can I cross the road now? _____

NO DOGS

7 I've got a dog. Can it come in? _____

PHONECARDS For Sale HERE

8 Excuse me, can we buy a phonecard here? _____

b `T5.1` Listen to the questions and answers. Practise saying them.

Articles: *a* and *the*

5 Write *a* or *the* in the correct places in the sentences, as in the examples.

a Can you ride ˢᵃ bicycle?

b Does it take ˢᵃ long time to get to ᵗʰᵉ centre of London?

c I always drive to work, but lot of people come by underground.

d Parking is real problem near my house.

e The traffic is very bad in evening.

f My uncle is train driver.

g Have you got car?

h We live in small town in United States.

6 In each sentence, one *the* is unnecessary. Cross it out, as in the example.

a Parking is very difficult in the city centre, so I always go there by ~~the~~ bus.

b Eight o'clock is a good time to phone Thomas: he is always at the home in the evening.

c It's so cold today that a lot of people can't go to the work.

d The train times are different on the Sundays.

e What do you think of the public transport in the London?

f You can use a Rail Card in most countries in the Europe.

g Do the people drive on the left in the United Arab Emirates?

h Our plane arrives in Los Angeles at the two o'clock in the afternoon.

most, a lot of, some, not many

7 Rearrange the words to make sentences.

a a bicycle – children – learn – Most – to ride

Most children learn to ride a bicycle.

b many – Not – on – people – Sundays – work

_____

c on holiday – British people – A lot of – go to Spain

_____

d can't – coffee – drink – without sugar – people – Some

_____

e lot of – flying – like – people – A – don't

_____

f Not many – understand – Japanese – European people – can

_____
_____

g enjoy – to tourists – Most – in my town – people – talking

_____
_____

h drive – night – at – Some – people – dangerously

_____

Listen and read

8 a **T5.2** Listen to and/or read the text about transport statistics.

Transport statistics

6	is the number of hours it takes to travel from London to New York by plane.
44	is the number of platforms at New York's Grand Central Terminal Station. Half a million people use the station every day.
209	kilometres an hour is the speed of the Spanish AVE train, which goes from the capital city Madrid to Seville, in the south of Spain, a distance of 470 km. The journey takes about two and a half hours.
567	is the number of passengers who can travel in a Boeing 747-400 aeroplane. It can fly for more than 12,000 kilometres without stopping. That's from London to Tokyo and back again.
9,297	kilometres is the distance of the Trans-Siberian railway, which goes from Moscow to the town of Vladivostok in eastern Russia. The journey takes seven days.
60,000	is the number of taxis in Mexico City.
6,000,000	is the total kilometres of roads in the United States.
43,000,000	is the number of people who travel through Heathrow Airport, near London, every year.

b Answer the questions about the text.

1 How long does it take to travel from Madrid to Seville by the AVE train?

Two and a half hours.

2 Where does the Trans-Siberian railway begin?

3 How many people can travel on a Boeing 747-400 aeroplane?

4 Which country has 6,000,000 kilometres of road?

5 How many people pass through Heathrow Airport every year?

6 Which city has 60,000 taxis?

7 Which railway station has 44 platforms?

8 How long does it take to fly from London to New York?

Real life
Catching planes and trains

9 **a** Make two dialogues with the sentences in the box.

That's £2.00.

Here's your boarding card. You're seat 25C.

When's the next train?

Which platform is it?

Gate 14, but your flight's delayed by one hour.

Which gate is it?

BA172 to Copenhagen. Here's my ticket.

Platform 3.

No, only hand luggage.

a At the check-in desk at an airport

CLERK: Good morning. Which flight are you on?

PASSENGER: (1) _____

CLERK: Have you got any luggage?

PASSENGER: (2) _____

CLERK: (3) _____

PASSENGER: (4) _____

CLERK: (5) _____

b At the ticket office in an underground station

PASSENGER: Hello, a single to Oxford Circus, please.

CLERK: (6) _____

PASSENGER: (7) _____

CLERK: They're every five minutes.

PASSENGER: (8) _____

CLERK: (9) _____

b **T5.3** Listen and check your answers.

31

Asking questions

10 Complete the questions with the verbs in the box.

Do	does	Can	Is	Has	Are	can	Have
~~are~~	do	does	is				

a   __Are__ trains crowded in Lisbon?

b   What time _____ people travel to work in Hong Kong?

c   _____ all the big cities in Germany got trams?

d   What time _____ the train leave in the morning?

e   _____ the traffic bad in Istanbul?

f   _____ Beijing got two airports?

g   _____ you drive from Moscow to St Petersburg in one day?

h   _____ they drive on the right in Malaysia?

i   How much _____ a flight from Bogotá to Rio de Janeiro?

j   Where _____ the Orient Express go to?

k   What colour _____ taxis in Singapore?

l   Where _____ I catch a taxi?

Pronunciation
The letter *a*

11 a **T5.4** Listen to the different ways we can pronounce the letter *a*.

/ɑː/	/eɪ/	/ɔː/	/æ/
artist	make	walk	catch
can't	_____	_____	_____
_____	_____	_____	_____
_____	_____	_____	_____

b Write these words in the correct column above.

~~can't~~	taxi	take	small
train	far	talk	traffic jam
car	travel	wait	football

c **T5.5** Listen to the words. Practise saying them.

Vocabulary booster
On a plane

12 a Match the words in the box with the things in the picture.

headphones	☐	a seatbelt	☐
an overhead locker	☐	a flight attendant	☐
an emergency exit	1	an aisle seat	☐
the aisle	☐	a passenger	☐
a sign	☐	a screen	☐
a window seat	☐	hand luggage	☐

b **T5.6** Listen and check. Practise saying the words.

Improve your writing
Completing an immigration form

13 Use the information below to complete Robert's immigration form.

AMERICAN *Airways*

YOUR FLIGHT DETAILS

For:	PRESTON/RMR
Booking Ref:	GSKTFM
Date of Flight:	THURSDAY,OCTOBER 15,04
From:	LIMA
To:	MIAMI
Airline:	AMERICAN AIRWAYS
Flight no:	AA9295

PASSPORT
UNITED KINGDOM OF GREAT BRITAIN AND NORTHERN IR

Name of bearer
Mr Robert Alexander PRESTON

National Status
UK CITIZEN

No. of passport
737935 G

Place of Birth
Eastbourne, East Sussex

Date of Birth
12 February 1983

P<GBRPRESTON<<ROBERT<ALEXANDER<<<<<<
000050749066GBR830212M080212<<<<<<<<<<<<<<

VISA WAIVER   Immigration

Type or print legibly with pen in ALL CAPITAL LETTERS. **USE ENGLISH.**

a Family name

b First (given) name

c Birth Date *(day / month / year)*

d Country of Citizenship

e Sex *(male or female)*

f Passport Number

g Airline and Flight Number

h Country where you live

i City where you boarded

CERTIFICATION: *I certify that I have read and understand all the questions and statements on this form. The answers I have furnished are true and correct to the best of my knowledge and belief.*

_____   _____

Signature   Date

Countable and uncountable nouns

1 a Ten of the words in the box are uncountable nouns. Circle them.

(butter) fruit meat water
tea journey cheese
hamburger egg vegetable
music bread food sugar
knife biscuit

b Choose the correct alternatives.

1 Check that the water *are* / *is* clean before you drink it.

2 The sugar *is* / *are* on the table.

3 The food in our hotel *aren't* / *isn't* very good. We eat all our *meal* / *meals* in a restaurant.

4 The journey from Miami to London *take* / *takes* about six hours.

5 Do you like *these* / *this* music? *It's* / *They're* by Mozart.

6 Everybody says that vegetables *are* / *is* very good for you.

7 *This* / *These* hamburgers *is* / *are* fantastic!

8 Fruit *isn't* / *aren't* expensive in my country.

Vocabulary
Food

2 In the word square, find:

Drinks	Types of fruit	Other things you can eat	
mineral water	*banana*	_____	_____
_____	_____	_____	_____
_____	_____	_____	_____
_____	_____	_____	_____
_____		_____	

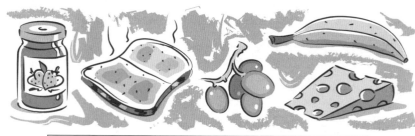

J	O	J	A	M	H	A	N	N	S	C	E
B	F	A	S	B	U	T	T	E	R	O	T
B	R	E	A	D	I	E	A	O	N	F	B
N	U	T	S	G	B	A	A	R	C	F	H
M	I	N	E	R	A	L	W	A	T	E	R
P	T	A	A	A	N	P	I	N	R	E	Y
T	J	P	I	P	A	I	C	G	C	T	O
A	U	P	N	E	N	Z	E	E	H	U	G
M	I	L	K	S	A	Z	M	M	E	E	H
R	C	E	G	G	S	A	E	H	E	I	U
C	E	R	E	A	L	T	O	A	S	T	R
S	A	U	S	A	G	E	S	M	E	N	T

there is / there are

3 Complete the sentences with the correct form of *there is* or *there are*.

a   ___Is there___ any milk in the fridge?

b   How many students _____ in your class?

c   _____ a very good beach near our hotel.

d   _____ any cheap restaurants near here?

e   _____ a university in Brighton?

f   I'm sorry, but _____ any shops open at this time.

g   _____ fifty states in the USA.

h   _____ any milk: how about lemon in your tea?

Short answers

LOOK!

> **Short answers with *there is* and *there are***
>
> **Is there a** hotel near here?   Yes, **there is.**
>   No, **there isn't.**
>
> **Are there any** good   Yes, **there are.**
> restaurants?   No, **there aren't.**

4 **a** Read about the campsite. Complete the questions, and write the correct short answer.

Las Molinas
Swimming pool
Tennis courts
Restaurant, drinks bar
Children's playground
10 km from the historic town of Los Pozos

1   ___Is___ there a swimming pool?
    ___Yes, there is.___

2   _____ there any places to eat and drink?
    _____

3   _____ there a beach?
    _____

4   _____ there a children's playground?
    _____

5   _____ there any supermarkets?
    _____

c **T6.1** Listen to the questions and short answers. Practise saying them.

some and any

5 Complete the sentences with *some* or *any*.

1   Have you got ___any___ orange juice?

2   There are _____ letters for you.

3   There's _____ salt, but there isn't _____ pepper.

4   We haven't got _____ eggs.

5   Would you like _____ milk in your coffee?

6   Are there _____ knives on the table?

7   We haven't got _____ more bread. Would you like _____ biscuits with your cheese?

8   I'm sorry, we haven't got _____ hot food, but we've got _____ sandwiches if you're hungry.

some, any, a(n) and no

6 **a** Complete the conversation in a sandwich shop with *some*, *any*, *a(n)* or *no*.

HELEN: I'd like (1) ___an___ egg sandwich, please.

ASSISTANT: OK, one egg sandwich ... butter?

HELEN: No, thanks, (2) _____ butter. I'm on (3) _____ diet.

ASSISTANT: OK ... here you are. Anything else with that? We've got (4) _____ very nice fruit ...

HELEN: Yes. (5) _____ apple, please.

ASSISTANT: OK, that's £2.50. And for you, sir?

CARLOS: Hmm. Have you got (6) _____ Swiss cheese?

ASSISTANT: No, sorry. There's (7) _____ Swiss cheese, but we've got (8) _____ English cheese, it's very good.

CARLOS: OK. (9) _____ cheese sandwich, please. Can I have (10) _____ salad with that?

ASSISTANT: Sure. Would you like (11) _____ drink?

CARLOS: Yes, (12) _____ bottle of mineral water, please.

b **T6.2** Listen and check. Practise saying the conversation.

Vocabulary booster
Vegetables and other things to eat

7 **a** Match the vegetables with the words in the box.

potatoes	☐	carrots	☐	onions	☐
cabbages	☐	beans	☐	peas	☐
tomatoes	☐	cucumbers	☐	lettuces	☐ 1
peppers	☐				

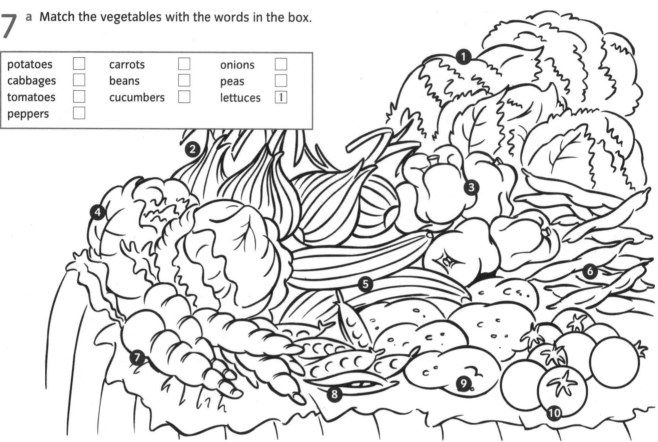

b T6.3 Listen and check. Practise saying the words.

c Label the pictures with the words in the box.

salad	crisps	~~salt~~	oil	French fries
vinegar	herbs	soy sauce		

1 _____salt_____   2 _____   3 _____   4 _____

5 _____   6 _____   7 _____   8 _____

d T6.4 Listen and check. Practise saying the words.

Listen and read

8 **T6.5** Read and listen to the recipe. Tick (✓) the correct picture.

A

B

C

D

Fish Cakes

Ingredients (to make 24 fish cakes):

500g boiled potatoes

350g cooked white fish

1 tablespoon tomato purée

2 tablespoons mixed herbs

50g breadcrumbs

a little oil

salt and pepper

Method:

1 Mash the boiled potatoes with a little salt and pepper.

2 Mix together the potatoes and the fish, tomato purée and herbs.

3 Add a little salt and pepper.

4 Make 24 fish cakes from the mixture. Cover the fish cakes with the breadcrumbs.

5 Heat the oil in a frying pan. Fry the fish cakes for about five minutes, turning them once.

6 Serve the fish cakes immediately with tomato sauce and a salad.

Questions with *how much* and *how many*

9 Complete the questions about the recipe, using *How much* or *How many*.

a A: _How many_ fish cakes does this recipe make?
 B: Twenty-four.

b A: _____ fish do you need?
 B: 350g.

c A: _____ potato do you use in the recipe?
 B: 500g.

d A: _____ tablespoons of herbs do you need?
 B: Two.

e A: _____ tomato purée do you add?
 B: 1 tablespoon.

f A: _____ oil do you use?
 B: A little.

g A: _____ grams of breadcrumbs do you need?
 B: Fifty.

h A: _____ minutes do you cook the fishcakes?
 B: About five.

Ordering food and drink

10 a Put the words in the correct order to make a dialogue in a restaurant.

A: order, – please – I – Can – your – take?

1 _Can I take your order, please?_____

B: have – Yes, – we – steaks – can – two

2 _____ ?

A: any – you – like – vegetables – Would?

3 _____ ?

B: please – some potatoes – and – Yes, – peas

4 _____

A: with – drink – Anything – that – to?

5 _____ ?

B: 'd – and a lemonade, – please – a mineral water – We – like

6 _____

b **T6.6** Listen and check. Practise saying the conversation.

Vocabulary
a cup of, a glass of, a bottle of

11 a Match the pictures to the words in the box.

a bag	☐
a bottle	☐
a carton	☐
a cup	☐
a glass	☐
a packet	☐

b Complete the phrases with the words in the box above.

1 a _bottle/glass_ of water

2 a _____ of milk

3 a _____ of sugar

4 a _____ of biscuits

5 a _____ of lemonade

6 a _____ of coffee

7 a _____ of orange juice

8 a _____ of tea

Pronunciation
Sentence stress

12 a (T6.7) Listen and underline the words which have the main sentence stress.

1 Can I have a bottle of mineral water, please?

2 You can catch a bus to the airport from here.

3 I always have orange juice with my breakfast.

4 What do you want for lunch?

5 I never drink coffee in the evening.

b Listen again and practise saying the sentences.

Improve your writing
Describing food

13 a Match the paragraphs to a nationality in the box.

Italian	☐	Mexican	☐	Argentinian	☐
Japanese	☐	French	☐	Hungarian	☐
Spanish	☐	British	☐		

1 Pizza is a very famous food from my country. Originally it comes from Naples, in the south of my country. A traditional pizza has cheese - mozzarella cheese - tomato and herbs. A lot of young people go to a pizza restaurant on Sunday evenings.
Andrea

2 A typical breakfast in my country is a very big cup of strong coffee, with lots of milk. The traditional thing to eat with your coffee is a croissant, maybe with butter or jam.
Jean-Christophe

3 People eat a lot of meat in my country, especially beef. On Sundays, people have a traditional lunch called an asado. In my family, my father cooks the meat on a barbecue, and we eat it with lots of salad
Oscar

4 The national dish of my country is gulyásleves. Many people think it's a meat dish but if you have real gulyás, it's a soup with lots of meat and vegetables.
Eva

b Write a few sentences about food in your country.

MODULE 7

Past Simple: was/were

1 Complete the sentences with was or were.

a My grandparents ___*were*___ married for more than fifty years.

b When I _____ in Berlin last year, the weather _____ very cold.

c How many people _____ there at the party?

d Where _____ you on Saturday evening?

e It _____ a beautiful day in August. My family and I _____ on holiday at the seaside.

f _____ George at school today?

g How _____ your first day at work?

h It _____ very nice to meet you, Mr Brown.

Short answers

2 **a** Read about the famous people on pages 39 and 40. Complete the questions and write the short answers.

Mark Twain
American writer
– born 1835
– died 1910

1 ___*Was*___ Mark Twain a painter?

___*No, he wasn't.*___

2 ___*Was*___ he American?

___*Yes, he was.*___

Charlie Chaplin
Film actor
– born London 1889
– died Switzerland 1977

3 _____ Charlie Chaplin born in America?

_____

4 _____ he an actor?

_____

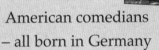

The Marx Brothers
American comedians
– all born in Germany

5 _____ the Marx Brothers born in the USA?

_____

6 _____ they comedians?

_____

Anna Pavlova
Russian dancer
– died 1931

7 _____ Anna Pavlova Russian?

_____

8 _____ she a singer?

_____

**Pelé
and Jaizinho**
Brazilian – the 1970
World Cup team

9 _____ Pelé and Jaizinho from Argentina?

_____

10 _____ they footballers?

_____

b **T7.1** Listen and check. Practise saying the questions and answers.

Vocabulary
Years, decades and centuries

3 Write the dates in full, as in the example.

a Disco music was very popular _in the nineteen-_
seventies. (1970–1979)

b The Athens Olympic Games were _____

_____ . (2004)

c Juan Peron was president of Argentina _____

_____ . (1946–1955)

d Elvis Presley was popular _____

_____ . (1950–1959)

e The Italian poet Dante was born _____

_____ . (1200–1299)

f Yugoslavia were world basketball champions

_____ . (1998)

g Abdul-Aziz was king of Saudia Arabia _____

_____ . (1932–1953)

h Catherine the Great was Empress of Russia _____

_____ . (1790–1799)

Past simple
Spelling of -ed endings

4 Write the Past simple tense of the verbs.

a like ___liked___ g play _____

b enjoy _____ h believe _____

c travel _____ i arrive _____

d study _____ j try _____

e look _____ k receive _____

f dance _____ l stay _____

Regular verbs

5 Complete the sentences with the Past simple of the verbs in the box.

graduate	study	change	try	start	die
work	end	live	help	walk	

a My brother ___graduated___ last year. He was at Glasgow University.

b The Second World War _____ in 1939, and

_____ six years later, in 1945.

c Elvis Presley, the King of Rock 'n' Roll,

_____ in 1977.

d There were no more buses, so I _____ home.

e When I was at school, my parents often

_____ me with my homework.

f I _____ French when I was at school, but I don't remember very much now.

g I _____ to phone you last night, but there was no answer.

h When he was a young musician, Reg Dwight

_____ his name to Elton John.

i The composer Chopin was born in Poland, but he

_____ in France for many years.

j I _____ in cinema for a big computer company in the nineties.

Irregular verbs

6 Complete the sentences with the past forms of the verbs in brackets.

Three child stars of the past

Mozart ...

a _wrote_ (write) music when he was five years old;

b _____ (leave) home when he was only twelve years old;

c _____ (go) to live in Vienna when he was 25 years old.

Wolfgang Amadeus Mozart – composer

Donny Osmond ...

d _____ (begin) singing on television at the age of five;

e _____ (sing) with his five brothers in the Osmond Brothers;

f _____ (sell) millions of records before he was 18.

Donny Osmond – pop star

Shirley Temple ...

g _____ (make) her first film when she was six;

h _____ (win) an Oscar in 1934;

i _____ (become) a politician in the 1970s.

Shirley Temple – actress

Prepositions of time

7 Complete the sentences with *at, from, in, on* or *to*.

a The economic situation in our country became much better ____*in*____ the 1990s.

b The café is open _____ 8.30 in the morning _____ about eleven o'clock in the evening.

c We arrived at the hotel _____ about eleven o'clock.

d We decided to have our holidays _____ September, when it's not so hot.

e _____ the age of seven, Vanessa started dancing lessons.

f I stayed at home _____ Friday because I had so much work to do.

g I was born _____ 1986.

h There was a war between the two countries _____ the nineteenth century.

Pronunciation
Past tense endings

8 a Look at the pairs of past forms below. Is the pronunciation of the underlined sounds the same (S) or different (D)?

1	bo<u>ugh</u>t	c<u>augh</u>t	_S_
2	wr<u>o</u>te	c<u>o</u>st	_D_
3	s<u>ai</u>d	r<u>ea</u>d	____
4	p<u>u</u>t	c<u>u</u>t	____
5	s<u>aw</u>	f<u>ou</u>nd	____
6	c<u>a</u>me	g<u>a</u>ve	____
7	l<u>o</u>st	c<u>o</u>st	____
8	t<u>oo</u>k	st<u>oo</u>d	____
9	w<u>o</u>re	c<u>augh</u>t	____
10	h<u>ea</u>rd	w<u>o</u>n	____

b **T7.2** Listen and check. Practise saying the words.

Past simple
Regular and irregular verbs

9 a **Complete the text about Amelia Earhart, using the correct form of the verbs.**

Seventy years ago, Amelia Earhart (1) ___was___ (be) America's favourite woman. In 1932, she (2) _____ (fly) across the Atlantic Ocean alone: the first woman to do this.

Her journey (3) _____ (start) in Newfoundland, Canada: fifteen hours later, her Lockheed Vega airplane (4) _____ (arrive) in Londonderry, Ireland. People all over the world (5) _____ (want) to meet this incredible woman. She (6) _____ (meet) King George V of England and (7) _____ (become) friends with the US President, Franklin D. Roosevelt. The American people (8) _____ (love) her.

Five years later, Amelia (9) _____ (try) to fly around the world. An American University (10) _____ (give) her $50,000 for a new Lockheed Electra airplane. On the morning of July 2nd 1937, Amelia and her co-pilot, Fred Noonan (11) _____ (leave) Lae, in New Guinea, and (12) _____ (begin) their journey to Howland Island in the Pacific Ocean.

On July 3rd 1937, the American ship *Itasca* (13) _____ (receive) a radio message from Amelia: a few minutes later her plane (14) _____ (disappear). American ships (15) _____ (spend) nearly two weeks looking for the plane, but they (16) _____ (find) nothing.

b **T7.3** Listen and check your answers.

Ordinal numbers

10 a **Write an ordinal number to complete the sentences. Use the numbers in brackets to help you.**

a Ronald Reagan was the ___fortieth___ President of the United States. (40)

b May is the _____ month in the year. (5)

c Our apartment is on the _____ floor. (8)

d Beethoven wrote his music in the _____ century. (19)

e Brazil won the World Cup for the _____ time in 1994. (4)

f The Berlin Wall fell near the end of the _____ century. (20)

g Neil Armstrong was the _____ man on the moon, and Buzz Aldrin was the _____ . (1/2)

h My sister's birthday is on the _____ of August. (22)

Dates

11 **Write the dates in full.**

a 5th Feb   ___February the fifth___

b 30th Jan   _____

c 17th Nov   _____

d 12th Aug   _____

e 21st Sep   _____

f 9th Apr   _____

Time phrases

12 Choose the correct time phrase.

a I go to the swimming pool *every week* / *last week*.

b I visited my friends in Canada *three years ago* / *every year*.

c My family lived in the United States *now* / *when I was a child*.

d We met Greg and Sonia *when we are on holiday* / *when we were on holiday*.

e I work in Slovenia *every summer* / *last summer*.

f We watched television *every evening* / *yesterday evening*.

g People usually to go university *when they are eighteen* / *when they were eighteen*.

h Jen spoke to her mother *every week* / *a week ago*.

Vocabulary booster
Common verbs

13 **a** Label the pictures on the right with the words in the box.

| break   build   catch   cut   fall   run   steal |
| throw   wake up   win |

b Here are the past forms of the verbs in the box. Write the infinitive forms.

1   broke   _break_

2   caught   _____

3   built   _____

4   threw   _____

5   woke up   _____

6   ran   _____

7   stole   _____

8   fell   _____

9   cut   _____

10 won   _____

c ▭**T7.4** Listen to the pronunciation of the infinitive and past forms. Practise saying them.

1 _____

2 _____

3 _break_____

4 _____

5 _____

6 _____

7 _____

8 _____

9 _____

10 _____

Listen and read

14 a **T7.5** Listen to and/or read the story of *The Strange Soldier*.

Manila

Mexico City

0   1000km
Scale

The Strange Soldier

It was a beautiful sunny morning in Mexico City. The date was October 10th, the year was 1593.

In the main square of the city, soldiers stood in front of the Royal Palace. The people of the city came and went as usual. But there was something strange about one of the soldiers: he wore a different uniform from the others, and had a different type of gun. When the other soldiers saw him, they began asking him questions. 'Who are you? Where are you from?' one of the other soldiers asked. 'I am a Spanish soldier,' he answered 'and because the governor died last night, it is my job to stay in front of the palace here.' 'The governor?' one of the soldiers replied, 'Which governor?' 'The governor of Manila, of course.'

The other soldiers told him he was in Mexico City – thousands of kilometres from the city of Manila.

The young soldier was amazed and had no idea how he came to be in a city so far from his home. Nobody believed his strange story. In the end, they put the young man in prison, and left him there until they decided what to do.

Two months later, a Spanish ship arrived from Manila. It brought news that the governor of Manila was dead – and the time of his death was 10 pm on the evening of October 9th, 1593. Was the young man's story true?

Four hundred years later, no one knows how it was possible for a man to travel across the world in one night ... without knowing how or why.

b Read the story again. Put these events in the order they happened.

A   The Mexican soldiers saw the strange soldier.   _____

B   The governor of Manila died.   __1__

C   They put the strange soldier in prison.   _____

D   A ship from Manila arrived in Mexico City.   _____

E   The strange soldier travelled from Manila to Mexico.   _____

Vocabulary
Life stories

15 Complete the information about Jed's life story. Look at page 66 of the Students' Book, if necessary.

I (a) w _a_ _s_ b _o_ _r_ _n_ in London in 1975. (b) A _ a c h _ _ _ I loved playing football and watching sport on television. I (c) w _ _ _ to s c _ _ _ _ in Chelsea and (d) w _ _ _ I w _ _ about nine I (e) b _ _ _ _ _ i n _ _ _ _ _ _ _ _ in computer games and the Internet. So I started a football website, which was very popular. I (f) l _ _ _ school when I was seventeen and I (g) s t _ _ _ _ _ computer design and mathematics at (h) u n _ _ _ _ _ _ _ _. When I (i) g r _ _ _ _ _ _ _ in 1997, I (j) g _ _ a j _ _ with a large computer games company and I (k) w _ _ _ to w _ _ _ in Chicago, in the United States. I (l) g _ _ m _ _ _ _ _ _ in 2000 to an American girl and now we've got our own family. Our two sons are football-crazy too!

Improve your writing
Time linkers: *before, after, then*

> **LOOK!**
>
> **Before** I went to bed, I phoned Suzanne.
> I phoned Suzanne **before** I went to bed.
>
> **After** Jane left university, she travelled to India.
> Jane travelled to India **after** she left university.
>
> Sebastian was a waiter in a restaurant. **Then** he found another job.

16 Join the sentences below with *before*, *after* or *then*.

a   _Before_ I went home, I bought something to eat from the supermarket.

b   _____ their dog died, the house was very quiet.

c   We had time for a coffee _____ the train left.

d   In the morning, I went shopping with my friend Sara. _____ we had lunch.

e   For a long time, nobody spoke. _____ someone asked a question.

f   _____ they got married, Paul and Linda usually stayed at home on Saturday nights.

g   _____ he was a famous actor, Bruce worked as a taxi driver.

h   I remembered to close all the windows _____ I went out.

MODULE 8

Vocabulary
Types of film

1 Match the types of film to the pictures.

cartoon	horror film	science fiction film
love story	action film	historical film
comedy	musical	

a   _love story_

b   _____

c   _____

d   _____

e   _____

f   _____

g   _____

h   _____

Adjectives to describe films

2 Find ten adjectives in the word square to describe films.

E	N	J	O	Y	A	B	L	E	D	O
X	O	A	N	B	M	L	A	F	U	S
C	R	O	I	O	S	O	F	V	S	I
I	N	T	E	R	E	S	T	I	N	G
T	H	R	A	I	N	I	P	O	S	A
I	F	U	N	N	Y	L	O	L	T	R
N	Z	S	P	G	Q	L	B	E	C	G
G	K	A	M	R	U	Y	C	N	Y	H
M	A	D	R	O	M	A	N	T	I	C
E	X	A	P	W	H	O	Y	V	D	J
F	R	I	G	H	T	E	N	I	N	G

Common verbs in the past tense

3 Complete the sentences with the past tense of the verbs in brackets,

a Martin Scorsese ____made____ (make) the film *Gangs of New York*.

b Lindsay's holiday last year _____ (cost) over €1000.

c Lucy's parents _____ (give) her a car for her 21st birthday.

d We were both so hot and thirsty that we _____ (drink) a litre bottle of mineral water.

e Steve _____ (become) a writer when he was forty-five.

f Karen's got a fantastic job – last month she _____ (earn) €3,000!

g The police looked everywhere for the money, but they only _____ (find) an empty bag.

h Jan and Anna _____ (fall) in love with each other at my birthday party two years ago.

i The first Spiderman film _____ (appear) in 2002.

j Last year we _____ (go) to the cinema a lot.

Past simple
Negative

4 Make the sentences negative.

a   We had good weather when we were on holiday.
We didn't have good weather when we were on holiday.

b   We went for a drive yesterday.
_____

c   Ben remembered to buy a birthday card.
_____

d   I heard the telephone.
_____

e   The letter arrived this morning.
_____

f   I ate in a restaurant last night.
_____

g   Amanda knew what to do.
_____

h   I checked my e-mail yesterday.
_____

Questions

5 Write questions about these famous people from the past.

a   Shakespeare / write / *Romeo and Juliet*
Did Shakespeare write 'Romeo and Juliet'?

b   Alexander Graham Bell / invent / e-mail
_____ ?

c   Marilyn Monroe / sing / *Candle in the Wind*
_____ ?

d   Captain Cook / discover / America
_____ ?

e   Leonardo da Vinci / paint / *Mona Lisa*
_____ ?

f   Madonna / play / *Evita*
_____ ?

g   Beethoven / write / rock songs
_____ ?

h   Laurel and Hardy / make / comedy films
_____ ?

i   Yuri Gagarin / travel / to the moon
_____ ?

Short answers

> **LOOK!**
>
> **Short answers with the Past simple**
>
> **Did** I/you/he/she/it/we/they know?
>
> **Yes,** I/you/he/she/it/we/they **did.**
> **No,** I/you/he/she/it/we/they **didn't**.

6 **a** Look again at the questions in exercise 5. Write the correct short answer for each question.

1   *Yes, he did.*
2   _____
3   _____
4   _____
5   _____
6   _____
7   _____
8   _____
9   _____

b **T8.1** Listen and check. Practise saying the questions and answers.

Question words

7 **a** A few days ago, Simon went on a business trip. Look at the papers in his wallet, and write questions about his day.

Eurolink

London - Paris	(SINGLE)
Departure time	14.30
Journey time	3 HOURS

The Station Buffet Restaurant

1 set menu   £14.50

+ SERVICE (10%)

Total £15.95

The Station Bookshop

Blue Guide to France   9.99
English–French Dictionary 4.99

BUREAU DE CHANGE

£200 changed to euros

1 ___*Where did he*_____ go?
   He went to Paris.

2 _____ travel?
   By train.

3 _____ have lunch?
   At The Station Buffet Restaurant.

4 _____ cost?
   £15.95.

5 _____ at the station?
   Some books.

6 _____ buy?
   Two.

7 _____ change?
   £200.

8 _____ leave?
   At 14.30.

9 _____ take?
   Three hours.

b **T8.2** Listen to the questions and answers. Practise saying them.

Past simple
Positive, negative and questions

8 Correct the sentences, as in the example.

a Did you ~~had~~ *have* a nice weekend?

b A: Did you see Alistair at the party?

   B: Yes, I saw.

c I didn't bought a newspaper yesterday.

d You listen to the news last night?

e A: Did you like the concert?

   B: No, I didn't like.

f When I was thirteen, I always wear jeans.

g You use my computer this afternoon?

h I didn't listened to my parents when I was young.

Pronunciation
Past forms

9 **a** **T8.3** Listen to the pronunciation of the past forms. Notice how the pronunciation of the underlined letters is the same.

/æ/ h<u>a</u>d, beg<u>a</u>n ___*drank*___ , _____ , _____

/e/ r<u>ea</u>d, f<u>e</u>ll _____ , _____

/ɔː/ c<u>au</u>ght, b<u>ou</u>ght _____ , _____ , _____

/ʌ/ c<u>u</u>t, sh<u>u</u>t _____

b What is the past form of the verbs in the box? Put them in one of the above groups according to the pronunciation of the past form.

~~drink~~	leave	meet	run	see	sing	think
wear	win					

c **T8.4** Listen to the pronunciation of the past forms of the verbs. Practise saying them.

Vocabulary booster
Books, magazines and newspapers

10 **a** Label the pictures with the words in the box.

headline	article	front page
newspaper	magazine	picture
advertisement	pages	cover
title	author	book

1 front page

2 newspaper

3 headline

DAILY NEWS
Newspaper of the Year

JANUARY 25th, 2001   www.daily.news.co.uk

WOMAN WITH A MISSION
BOB JOHNSON'S NATIONWIDE QUEST FOR FEMALE FINANCIAL ADVICE

New sales blow hits Superstores

Poor Christmas profits deepen gloom for Superstore

By Tom Barley

INSIDE: JERRY WILSON 4-5 • SHOPPING 11 • SHARES & MARKET PRICES 12-13

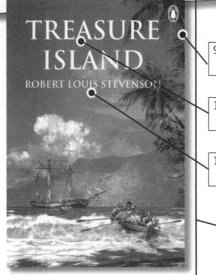

4 article

5 magazine

6 picture

7 pages

The Image

WHAT'S HOT THIS SUMMER

Now the nights are getting lighter, it's time to turn on the heat. No problem – just grab a brush and comb and style you hair to these ten styles...

Hair styles this summer are the hottest we've seen for ages. Treat yourself to a look that will turn heads.

YOUR LETTERS

8 Advertisement

FASHION NEWS FROM NEW YORK

New! **Silver Shine** Nail Varnish

page 12

9 book

10 title

11 author

12 cover

TREASURE ISLAND
ROBERT LOUIS STEVENSON

b T8.5 Listen and check. Practise saying the words.

Listen and read

11 a **T8.6** Listen and/or read about this hero and heroine.

National heroes and heroines

Mustafa Kemel Atatürk

Mustafa Kemal Atatürk is the father of modern Turkey. He was born in 1881. He chose the army as a career and in 1915, during the First World War, he led the Turkish army at Gelibolu and Istanbul. By the end of the war he was a hero and from that time on all of the Turkish people supported him. He led the Turkish army in the War of Independence (1919–1922) and in 1923 he became the first President of the new Republic of Turkey. During the last fifteen years of his life Atatürk introduced many reforms and did many things to improve life in Turkey. He died in November 1938, but today the people of Turkey still think of him with great respect.

Florence Nightingale

A hundred and fifty years ago, most nurses did not study nursing: but a British woman called Florence Nightingale tried to change all that. In the 1850s, she worked in a hospital for wounded soldiers in the Crimea (now Ukraine). People say she never slept, but spent all her time helping the men. The soldiers called her 'The Lady of the Lamp' because of the lamp she always carried as she walked around at night. When she returned to England, she began a school of nursing in London. She died in 1910.

Glossary   Gelibolu = Gallipoli   wounded = hurt in a battle or war

b Write the questions for the answers, as in the example.

1   _When was Mustafa Kemal Ataturk born?_
In 1881.

2   _____
_____
_____
He led the Turkish army at Gelibolu and Istanbul.

3   _____
_____
In 1923.

4   _____
_____
_____
In 1938.

5   _____
_____
_____
In the 1850s.

6   _____
_____
_____
'The Lady of the Lamp'.

7   _____
_____
_____
When she returned to England.

Arranging a night out

12 Choose the correct alternative.

DAVID: Joe, (a) *do* / *would* / *are* you want to go out tomorrow night?

JOE: Okay, but I (b) *don't* / *haven't* / *didn't* got much money.

DAVID: Well, (c) *we* / *do we* / *let's* go to the cinema.

JOE: Okay. What's (d) *on* / *at* / *in*?

DAVID: (e) *There's* / *It's got* / *There are* a new film by Ang Lee.

JOE: Great! I saw his last film – it (f) *was* / *were* / *did* fantastic!

DAVID: Why (g) *we don't* / *don't we* / *can't we* have a pizza first?

JOE: Okay, that's (h) *a* / *the* / *—* good idea.

Improve your writing
A diary

13 **a** Ray is a young Australian on holiday in Europe. He decided to travel from London to Prague by bus. Complete his holiday diary with the phrases in the box.

a ~~in the evening~~	e was in another country
b the bus wasn't there	f and listened to the music
c only cost £50	g we finally left London
d When we arrived in France	h I walked back to the car park

Sunday

Today was my last day in London. I spent the afternoon walking around, and (1) __a__ I met two of my friends in a place called the Southern Lights, near Victoria Station. We talked (2) _____ . I felt sorry to leave London, but everybody says Prague is a really beautiful city. I went home early – about ten o'clock – and packed my suitcase for tomorrow. London to Prague is 22 hours on the bus – it's a long journey, but my ticket (3) _____ .

Monday

We left Victoria Coach Station at about 1 o'clock. The bus was full of people, mostly young. There were one or two Australians! The traffic was really bad at that time and it was nearly an hour before (4) _____ . We arrived in Dover in the afternoon and took the ferry across the English Channel. (5) _____ they asked to see my passport … and then they told me I needed to pay for a visa!!

Tuesday

I fell asleep somewhere in the north of France … I felt so tired and when I woke up I (6) _____ !! The motorway was full of big German cars and everybody drove at about 150 kph!! About 10 o'clock, we stopped at a motorway service station, and I went into the shop for something to eat and drink. Twenty minutes later, (7) _____ . Life was good: I had food, drink and it was only four more hours to Prague. There was only one problem … (8) _____ !!

b Complete Ray's diary with the verbs in the box.

~~were~~	drove	opened	sat
spoke	thought	got	
stopped	helped	saw	
started	said	remembered	
told	~~was~~		

I was in a complete panic. My bag, my clothes and my passport (1) __were__ all on the bus, the bus (2) __was__ on the motorway … and I was at the motorway service station. I (3) _____ down by the road, thinking, 'What can I do? Help!!' And soon someone (4) _____ me. A kind German woman – who (5) _____ perfect English – asked me if there was a problem. I (6) _____ her about the bus, and she (7) _____ she could help me. We (8) _____ into her big German car – it was a Mercedes – and we (9) _____ along the motorway at about 180 kilometres an hour.

A few minutes later, we (10) _____ the bus – my bus. My new German friend (11) _____ her window and (12) _____ shouting 'Stop!! Stop!!' at the bus driver (in German, of course!!).

At first, the bus driver (13) _____ she was crazy and drove faster … until he saw me. Perhaps he (14) _____ my face. Then we drove along together until the next motorway service station, and then we both (15) _____ .

Adjectives
Opposites

1 Write the opposite of the following things.

a   an expensive hotel

   a cheap hotel

b   a difficult question

   _____

c   a big country

   _____

d   an attractive face

   _____

e   an old bicycle

   _____

f   a comfortable chair

   _____

g   a slow train

   _____

Comparative adjectives

2 Add the correct letters to make the comparative form of the adjectives.

a   young _er_

b   eas _i er_

c   big _g er_

d   cheap _er_

e   health _i er_

f   new _er_

g   happ _i er_

h   slim _mer_

i   quiet _er_

j   hot _ter_

3 **a** Read the two facts, then write a sentence using the comparative form of the adjective.

1   The area of Brazil is 8.5 million km².
   The area of Australia is 7.6 million km².
   Brazil is bigger than Australia.

   _____ (big)

2   The River Volga in Russia is 3,500 km long.
   The River Mississippi in the USA is 6,000 km long.

   _____
   _____ (long)

3   Blue whales usually weigh about 130 tonnes.
   Elephants usually weigh about 7 tonnes.

   _____
   _____ (heavy)

4   The Pyramids in Egypt are about 4,000 years old.
   The Parthenon in Greece is about 2,500 years old.

   _____
   _____ (old)

5   The Eiffel Tower in Paris is 324 m tall.
   The Sears Tower in Chicago is 443 m tall.

   _____
   _____ (tall)

6   The Akashi-Kaikyo Bridge in Japan is nearly 2,000 m long.
   The Sydney Harbour Bridge in Australia is 500 m long.

   _____
   _____ (long)

7   The price of gold is about $8,000 per kilo.
   The price of silver is about $150 per kilo.

   _____
   _____ (expensive)

8   English has more than a hundred irregular verbs.
   Esperanto has no irregular verbs!

   _____
   _____ (easy)

b T9.1 Listen to the sentences. Practise saying them.

Superlative adjectives

4 **a** Read the information about the Olympic athletes below.

Roy Seagrove -
Rower

Age: 38
Height: 1 m 90
Weight: 95 kg
These are his fifth
Olympic Games
Three Olympic
medals up to now

Jim Bowen -
Basketball player

Age: 19
Height: 1 m 95
Weight: 89 kg
First Olympic Games
Started playing
basketball three
months ago

Jake Kay -
Marathon runner

Age: 25
Height: 1 m 60
Weight: 51 kg
Silver medal in the
last Olympics

Karina Green -
Swimmer

Age: 16
Height: 1 m 72
Weight: 57 kg
First Olympic Games

b Complete the sentences as in the example.

1 _Roy Seagrove_ is _the oldest._____ (old)

2 _____ is _____ . (young)

3 _____ has got _____ hair. (long)

4 _____ has got _____ hair. (short)

5 _____ is _____ . (tall)

6 _____ is _____ . (heavy)

7 _____ is _____ . (small)

8 _____ is _____ . (successful)

5 Change the adjective into the superlative form. Can you answer the questions?

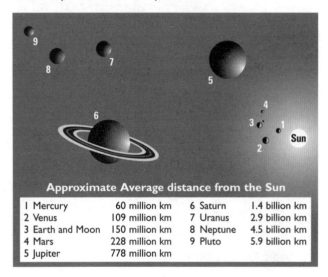

Approximate Average distance from the Sun

1 Mercury	60 million km	6 Saturn	1.4 billion km
2 Venus	109 million km	7 Uranus	2.9 billion km
3 Earth and Moon	150 million km	8 Neptune	4.5 billion km
4 Mars	228 million km	9 Pluto	5.9 billion km
5 Jupiter	778 million km		

a Which is _the nearest___ (near) planet to the Sun?

Mercury

b What's the _____ (small) planet?

_____

c This planet has got over thirty moons and it's

_____ (big) planet in the solar system.

_____

d Which is _____ (hot) planet?

_____

e This is the _____ (far) planet from the

Sun, and also _____ (cold).

_____

f Which planet is _____ (easy)

to see from Earth?

_____

g Which planet is _____ (close) to

Earth?

_____

Comparative and superlative adjectives

6 a Complete the joke with the comparative or superlative forms of the adjectives.

A woman went into (1) <u>*the most expensive*</u> (expensive) butcher's in town and asked for (2) _____ (big) chicken in the shop. The shopkeeper showed her a chicken and said 'This is (3) _____ (good) chicken in the shop, madam.' 'It's very small,' she said. 'Have you got a (4) _____ (large) one?' 'Just a moment,' said the shopkeeper. He took the chicken into another room. In fact it was the only chicken he had. So he put some sausages inside to make it look (5) _____ (big).
'Here you are,' he said. 'This is our (6) _____ (delicious) chicken. And you can see that it's (7) _____ (big) than the other. But I'm afraid it's also (8) _____ (expensive).'
'Hmm ... but I'm not sure if it's (9) _____ (good) than the other. OK. Can I have both of them, please?'

b **T9.2** Listen to the joke and check your answers.

Pronunciation
Comparatives

7 a **T9.3** Listen to the comparative adjectives. Notice the pronunciation of *than*. Practise saying them.

bigger than	older than
faster than	more expensive than
slower than	more difficult than

b **T9.4** Listen to the sentences. Tick (✓) the true ones and cross (✗) the false ones. Then practise saying them.

1 ☐ 2 ☐ 3 ☐ 4 ☐ 5 ☐ 6 ☐

One and ones

8 Rewrite the sentences, changing the word in bold to *one* or *ones*.

a I don't have my old car now. I bought a new **car** last week.
I bought a new <u>*one last week.*</u>

b Martha has got three children. The youngest **child** is nearly three.
The youngest _____ .

c Your shoes are much more expensive than the **shoes** I bought.
Your shoes are much more expensive than _____
_____ .

d 'Which colour pen would you like?'
'The red **pen**, please.'
The red _____ .

e There are many old buildings in the town centre. These **buildings** are the oldest.
These _____ .

Vocabulary
Shops and shopping

9 a Rearrange the letters to make the names of shops. Look at page 82 of the Students' Book, if necessary.

1 You can buy steak at a <u>*butcher's*</u> . BRUSHTEC'

2 You can buy shirts, trousers and skirts at a _____ . LOSHCET POSH

3 You can buy bread at a _____ . YKERAB

4 You can buy stamps and send parcels at a _____ . STOP COFFEI

5 You can buy medicine at a _____ . SHARMYCAP

6 You can have a haircut at a _____ . DERRAHISSER'

7 You can buy a present at a _____ . FIGT OHPS

8 You can buy newspapers and food and household items at a _____ . CALLO HOPS

9 You can take your clothes for cleaning at a _____ . RYD SERCANEL'

b **T9.5** Listen and check your answers. Practise saying the sentences.

Listen and read

10 **T9.6** Listen and/or read about three machines you can buy to make your life easier.

Which machine is ...

a   the most useful? <u>the Bryson D838 Robot Vacuum Cleaner</u>

b   the cheapest? _____

c   the most useful for cooking ideas? _____

d   the most expensive? _____

e   the smallest? _____

f   the best one for people who hate housework? _____

The three most intelligent machines for your home...

Thanks to computer chips, you can now buy machines that can think!! Here are some of the best machines which can really make your life easier.

The Bryson D838 Robot Vacuum Cleaner

Do you like housework? No? Then this new robot vacuum cleaner is the machine for you. It can clean your living room automatically. It has a computer which tells it to go around objects such as chairs and table legs as it cleans your floor. And if a person – or your pet dog or cat – comes too close, it stops automatically. The Bryson D838 Robot Vacuum Cleaner comes with electric batteries, and costs £1,800.

The Freezolux Smart Fridge

 A fridge which tells you what it's got inside ... and gives you ideas about what to cook for dinner!! A visual display shows you what's inside the fridge – you don't even have to open the door, and the fridge can also tell when food is too old to use. And if you haven't got any ideas about what to cook for your family this evening ... just touch the computer screen on the door of the fridge, and you can look at over a thousand of your favourite recipes. You can also use it to send e-mails and to surf the Internet. The Freezolux Smart Fridge is more than just a fridge and costs only £999!

The Ultimate Power Control System

How many remote control units do you have in your house ... for the TV, the video, the CD player ... now you can control everything in your house – from a light in the bedroom to your front door – using just one special remote control unit. It works with radio signals so you can do everything in your house without getting out of bed. You can even surf the Internet, send e-mails, watch videos or listen to a CD with the Ultimate Power Control System's video screen. Price – £45. Buy now!!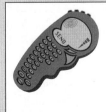

Improve your writing
Describing a place

11 **a** Complete the text about *My Favourite Shop* with the phrases in the box.

> The best time to go is   is open
> ~~My favourite shop is~~   it sells
> until eight o'clock at night
> The reason I like it is
> The people there

My Favourite Shop

(1) <u>My favourite shop is</u> called Talad Thai. It's in Putney, in south London. It's next to a Chinese restaurant, and

(2) _____ all kinds of food from China, Thailand and many other countries in the Far East.

(3) _____ because I love cooking, especially Oriental food. The shop (4) _____ seven days a week, from ten o'clock in the morning

(5) _____ .

(6) _____ on a Sunday morning, when the shop is usually very quiet.

(7) _____ are always very friendly and they always try to help you find what you want.

b Write a similar paragraph about a shop you know. Write about:

- what it is called
- where it is
- what it sells
- why you like it
- opening times
- the best time to go there
- the people there

Vocabulary booster
A supermarket

12 **a** Label the things in the picture with the words in the box.

checkout   cashier   shopping list   customer   shopping trolley shopping basket   ~~till~~   queue   cans   plastic bags

1 _____

2 _____

3 till

4 _____

5 _____

6 ....

7 _____

8 _____

9 _____

10 _____

b (T9.7) Listen and check. Practise saying the words.

Asking in shops

13 a Write the conversations in full.

1 A: Sell / sausages?

Do you sell sausages?

B: Yes / the Food Hall

_____

A: Which floor / that?

_____ ?

B: It / on / ground floor

It's on ground floor

2 A: Have / got / these shoes / size 38?

_____ ?

B: What colour / you / like?

_____ ?

A: Black / brown

_____

3 A: Can / buy / these, please?

_____ ?

B: That / £49.99

_____

A: you / take / credit cards?

_____ ?

B: Yes, visa / mastercard

_____

4 A: Can / have / one / those, please?

_____ ?

B: One / these?

_____ ?

A: Yes. How much / it?

_____ ?

B: It / 75p

_____

5 A: What time / supermarket / close?

_____ ?

B: We / open / all night

_____

b **T9.8** Listen and check. Practise saying the conversations.

Possessives

Possessive adjectives	Possessive pronouns
my	mine
your	yours
his	his
her	hers
its	its
our	ours
their	theirs

LOOK!

a We use a possessive adjective when there is a noun after it.

*Is this **your book**?*

We use a possessive pronoun when there is no noun after it.

*Is this book **yours**? No, it's **hers**.*

b We can use names with a noun or without a noun.

*That's **Pete's** bag. That's **Pete's**.*

14 Correct the words in bold.

a A: Is this ~~Scott~~ mobile? ___*Scott's*___

B: No, it's **Julia**. _____

b **You** watch is newer than **my**. _____

_____

c Where's Liz **Gardener** office? Is this **she** computer?

_____ _____

d The Gates family live in that house. That car is

their. _____

e **Us** best-selling camera is the XP40. _____

f Where's David? I think these car keys are **him**.

_____

g This is our new model coupe. **It** top speed is 200

kilometres an hour. _____

h This dress was Marilyn **Monroe**. These sunglasses

were **she** too. _____ _____

i Oh no! I think that bus was **our**! _____

j A: Whose pen is this?

B: It's **Tony**. _____

A: No, it's **I**. _____

Spelling
-ing forms

1 Write the -ing form of the verbs.

a read _____reading_____

b study _studying_

c wash _washing_

d leave _leving_

e come _coming_

f stop _stopping_

g look _cooking_

h dance _dancing_

i stay _staing_

j give _giving_

k plan _planning_

l write _writing_

Present continuous

2 **a** Look at the picture on the right. Write what the people are doing, using the verbs.

1 The robot ___is cleaning___ (clean) the living room.

2 Veronica _is looking_ (look) out of the window.

3 She _____ (talk) to someone on her mobile phone.

4 The baby _is sitting_ (sit) on the floor.

5 The baby _____ (eat) the flowers.

6 Ronald _____ (have) a cup of tea.

7 He _____ (watch) television.

8 The two older children _are doing_ (do) their homework.

b **T10.1** Listen and check. Practise saying the sentences.

Question words

3 **a** Write the correct question words in the following sentences and match them to their answers below.

1 ___What___ are you doing? [f]

2 _____ are you going? [d]

3 _____ are you smiling? [a]

4 _____ are you talking to? [b]

5 _____ are you reading? [c]

6 _____ are you watching? [e]

a Because you look so funny!

b My brother.

c Oh, nothing, just a magazine.

d To my English class.

e Ssh!! It's my favourite programme.

f My homework.

b **T10.2** Listen to the questions and answers. Practise saying them.

Short answers

Short answers with the Present continuous

Are you going home?
Yes, **I am/we are**.
No, **I'm/we're not**.

Are they going home?
Yes, **they are**.
No, **they aren't**.

Is he/she listening?
Yes, **he/she is**.
No, **he/she isn't**.

Notice: We do not use contracted forms in **positive** short answers.

Yes, I am. **not** ~~*Yes, I'm.*~~

4 Write short answers.

a   Are you enjoying the party, Jo?

Yes, _____ I am. _____

b   Is it raining outside?

No, _____ .

c   Are your friends staying in this hotel?

Yes, _____ .

d   Are you two coming with us?

Yes, _____ .

e   Are you waiting to see the doctor?

No, _____ .

f   Is Thomas driving?

Yes, _____ .

g   Is she talking to us?

No, _____ .

All forms

5 a Put the verbs in brackets into the correct form of the Present Continuous: positive, negative, question form or short answer.

SOPHIE: It's me, Sophie.

JENNY: Hi, Sophie. Where are you? What (1) ___ *are you doing* ___ (you do)?

SOPHIE: I'm at my sister's wedding.

JENNY: Fantastic! (2) _____ (you enjoy) yourself?

SOPHIE: No, (3) _____ !! (4) _____ (I not have) a good time. It's awful!!

JENNY: Why? What (5) _____ (happen)?

SOPHIE: Well, there's the music for a start. (6) _____ (They play) this awful 80s music ... and ... oh no, I don't believe it ... My dad (7) _____ (dance) with my mum's sister.

JENNY: How about your mum? (8) _____ (she dance) too?

SOPHIE: No, (9) _____ . (10) _____ (She not do) anything. (11) _____ (She look) at my dad.

JENNY: Oh dear!!

SOPHIE: Just a minute ... there's a very nice young man over there. There's a girl talking to him but (12) he _____ (not listen) ... and ... oh!!

JENNY: Sophie. What (13) _____ (he do)?

SOPHIE: He (14) _____ (come) over ... Talk to you later ... 'Bye!!

b **T10.3** Listen to the conversation and check your answers.

homework

Present continuous and Present simple

6 Underline the best form of the verb, Present simple or Present continuous.

a A: Can I speak to Jane Parsons, please?

  B: Sorry, she's not in the office today. *She works /* (*She's working*) at home today.

b A: Where *do you come / are you coming* from?

  B: I'm Italian ... from Milan.

c A: *Do you speak / Are you speaking* Japanese?

  B: Just a little.

d Don't forget your umbrella! *It's raining / It rains* again.

e A: Can you help me with the dinner?

  B: Not now ... *I watch / I'm watching* TV.

f In Britain, people *drive / are driving* on the left.

g A: Hello!! What *do you do / are you doing* here?

  B: *I'm waiting / I wait* for a friend.

h Can I look at the newspaper now? *Are you reading / Do you read* it?

i Can I phone you back later? *We're having / We have* dinner.

Vocabulary
Clothes

7 Look at the pictures of Bob, Paul and Marie. Who is wearing ...

a trainers? — Bob

b a skirt? — Marie

c a coat? — Bob

d a tie? — Paul

e black shoes? — Paul

f earrings? — Marie

g a shirt? — Paul

h jeans? — Bob

i a suit? — Paul

j trousers? — Paul

k a white jacket? — Marie

l a pullover? — Bob

Bob

Paul

Marie

Describing people

8 Match the definitions to the words.

a a piece of jewellery that you wear on your ear — 7

b a head where all – or nearly all – the hair is cut — 5

c the hair on a man's face under his mouth — 10

d attractive: nice to look at — 3

e (for a person) the opposite of small or short — 1

f thin, in a good way — 9

g you wear these if you can't see very well — 4

h hair which is yellow or light-coloured — 6

i you use them to see things — 12

j the hair on a man's face above his mouth — 11

k hair which is brown or black — 2

l hair which you tie together at the back of your head — 8

1 tall

2 dark

3 good-looking

4 glasses

5 shaved

6 blonde

7 ~~earring~~

8 ponytail

9 slim

10 beard

11 moustache

12 eyes

Listen and read

9 [T10.4] Listen to and/or read about street style, and complete the table.

	Where is she from?	What clothes does she talk about?	Where did she buy her clothes?
Mina	London		
Gloria		dress, trousers, shoes	
Alice			Milan, New York

Street Style

This week we went to South Molton Street to find out what young people are wearing when they go shopping.

◆ **Site Map**

News

Chat room

Horoscopes

e-mail

Mina is from London: she's a student at the London College of Fashion.

'I'm wearing a pair of jeans from *Michiko* – it's a Japanese shop here in London.' 'I love Japanese clothes. The jumper is from *Space*, and I bought the jacket at Camden Market a couple of weeks ago. My bag and shoes were presents from my family. I like wearing clothes that are different, so I don't usually go shopping in big shops.'

Gloria is a designer from Barcelona, in Spain. She's spending a few days here in London. 'Because I'm a designer, I love making clothes for myself. I made this dress, and these trousers, too. My shoes are from Spain, too ... they're my favourite shoes, but I can't remember where I bought them!'

'I'm looking for a bag which looks good with these clothes. I love shopping in London, but it's very expensive!'

Alice is from the United States. She works for an airline company. 'I travel a lot because of my job: I love my work because I can go shopping in lots of wonderful places.'

'I bought this top in Milan, and my trousers and shoes are from New York. As well as Italy and the United States, I love shopping here in London, too. I'm going to a shop called *Puzzle* – it's near here – to buy myself a new jacket.'

's

10 **a** Write *'s* in the correct place in the sentences.

1 My sister*'s* in her mid-twenties.

2 Everybody says she *'s* very good-looking.

3 Where *'s* Frank going?

4 Who *'s* the girl with long hair?

5 Dina *'s* got short hair.

6 David *'s* mother doesn't wear glasses.

7 Ann *'s* the black girl with medium-length hair.

8 Maria *'s* waiting for me in the car.

b Does *'s = is, has* or possessive in each sentence?

1 _____	4 _____	7 _____
2 _____	5 _____	8 _____
3 _____	6 _____	

Real Life
Street talk

homework

11 **a** Write the words in the box in the correct place in the sentences.

~~here~~ do it this to the

a Is anyone sitting /*here*?

b Excuse me, have you got /*the* time, please?

c Is this bus going /*to* the city centre?

d Is /*it* okay to park here?

e Is /*this* the way to the station?

f What time /*do* the shops close on Saturdays?

b Match the sentences to the answers.

1 It's half past two. [b]

2 No, you can't park here. [d]

3 At one o'clock. [f]

4 No, it's free. [a]

5 Yes, it's over there. [e]

6 No, you need the number 23 over there. [c]

Improve your writing
Correcting mistakes

12 Read the description of the picture. Correct the twelve underlined mistakes.

There (a) <u>is</u> *are* five people in the picture. They are all (b) <u>siting</u> outside: it's a nice day and the sun is (c) <u>shineing</u> *t*. Perhaps they (d) <u>is</u> all on holiday together. One of the men is (e) <u>wearring</u> *are* a suit. One man is behind the others: (f) <u>she's</u> *he's* reading a book. The woman in the front (g) <u>have</u> *he's* got a newspaper, but she (h) <u>don't</u> *has* reading it. Her (i) <u>eye</u> are closed: perhaps (j) <u>she</u> *isn't* sleeping. I like this picture: the people (k) <u>looks</u> *is* calm and happy and the scenery is very (l) <u>atractive</u>.

Pronunciation
Stress in questions

13 **T10.5** Listen to the pronunciation of the question words, and the questions with the Present continuous.

1	What	What are you doing?
2	What	What are they doing?
3	What	What's he doing? What's she doing?
4	Where	Where are you going?
5	Where	Where are they going?
6	Where	Where's he going? Where's she going?

b Listen again and practise saying the questions.

MODULE 11

can/can't for ability

1 a Look at the information about four students: Caroline, Fabrizio, Kristina and Max.

Caroline

Fabrizio

Kristina

Max

	speak French	play chess	drive a car	play a musical instrument
Caroline	✓	✗	✗	✓
Fabrizio	✓	✓	✗	✗
Kristina	✗	✗	✓	✓
Max	✗	✓	✓	✗

b Complete the sentences about Caroline and Fabrizio.

1 Caroline ___*can*___ speak French.
2 She ___*can't*___ play chess.
3 _____ drive a car.
4 _____ play a musical instrument.
5 Fabrizio _____
6 He _____
7 _____
8 _____

c 〔 T11.1 〕 Listen to the sentences. Practise saying them.

Questions and short answers

> **Short answers with can/can't**
>
> **Can** I/you/he/she/we/they **ask a question?**
>
> **Yes,** I/you/he/she/we/they **can.**
>
> **No,** I/you/he/she/we/they **can't.**

2 a Look back at the information about Kristina and Max. Write the questions and short answers.

1 *Can Kristina speak French?*
   No, she can't.

2 _____
   _____

3 _____
   _____

4 _____
   _____

5 _____
   _____

6 _____
   _____

7 _____
   _____

8 _____
   _____

b 〔 T11.2 〕 Listen to the questions and answers. Practise saying them.

Question words

3 Complete the questions with the correct question word(s) in the box.

| Where   How long   How |
| What time   What kind |
| What colour   What   When |
| How well   Which |

a   A: _Where_ is Brisbane?

   B: It's in Australia.

b   A: _what kind_ of tree is that?

   B: It's a palm tree.

c   A: _When_ did you go to South America?

   B: Four years ago.

d   A: _Which_ is your coat?

   B: The long black one.

e   A: _How long_ was the film?

   B: Two and a half hours.

f   A: _what colour_ is your new car?

   B: White.

g   A: _what time_ do we arrive in New York?

   B: At about three o'clock.

h   A: _What_ 's your sister's name?

   B: Maria.

i   A: _How_ do I switch this off?

   B: Press the red button.

j   A: _How well_ can you type?

   B: I can't type!

4 a Read the text below.

Ships of the desert

Perhaps they aren't the most beautiful animals in the world ... but in the hot lands of North Africa and the Middle East they are certainly one of the most useful. But how much do you know about camels?

Camels normally live for about 40 years – but they usually stop working when they are about 25.

Camels don't normally like running – it's too hot – but when they need to, they can run at 20 kilometres an hour. The dromedary, or Arabian camel, has one hump. The Bactrian, or Asian camel, has longer hair and has got two humps. There are about 14 million camels in the world, and most of them are dromedaries.

An adult camel is about 2.1 metres tall and weighs about 500 kilograms. Camels can walk for more than 600 kilometres without drinking. They only need to drink water every six or eight days. But when there is water, they can drink up to 90 litres.

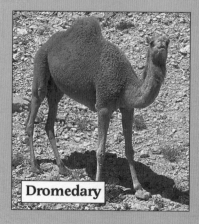

Dromedary

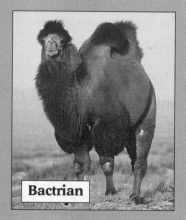

Bactrian

b Write the questions for this information.

1 _How long do camels live?_
For about forty years.

2 How _fast can they run?_
About twenty kilometres an hour.

3 How _many humps does a dromedary have?_
One.

4 How _many camels are there in th'world?_
14 million.

5 How _tall is an adult camels?_
2.1 metres.

6 How _much does an adult camel weighs?_
About 500 kilograms.

7 How _for can camels walk without drinking?_
More than 600 kilometres.

8 How _often camel do need to drink water?_
Every six or eight days.

9 How _mach water they drink water?_ can
Up to ninety litres.

5 Complete the sentences with How much, How many, Which or What.

a _What_ do you study at university?

b _How many_ aunts and uncles have you got?

c There's chocolate or vanilla ice cream for dessert.
Which do you prefer?

d _How much_ milk do you want in your coffee?

e There's a bus at nine o'clock and another one at eleven o'clock. _Which_ is better for you?

f _How much_ time did you spend in Africa?

g _How many_ people were there at the meeting?

h _How much_ does a kilo of cheese cost?

i _What_ is the capital of Romania?

Word order in questions

6 Put the words in the correct order to make questions.

a are there / in / How / many / the USA / states?
How many states are there in the USA?

b did / films / How many / make / he ?
How many films did he make?

c a football match / does / How / last / long?
How long does a football much last?

d the boxer / Muhammad Ali / born / was / Where?
Where was the boxer Muhmmad Ali born?
How

e it from / How far / here / to your home / is?
How far is your home for me here?

f do / of / What kind / like / you / music?
What kind music do you like? of

g can / a / cheetah / fast / run /How?
How fast can cheetah run? a

h the world / is / in / the biggest / ocean / What?
what is the biggest ocean in thword?

Questions with other verb forms

7 Complete the questions with the verbs in the box.

were	can	is	did	was	~~are~~	did	do

a Where _are_ my glasses?

b How _did_ you get to school this morning?

c How often _____ you go to the cinema?

d How fast _____ the Toyota?

e How many people _____ there at the party last night?

f How many languages _____ you speak?

g When _____ you start learning English?

h Who _____ president in 1978?

65

Vocabulary booster
Animals

8 **a** How many of the animals below can you name?
Write the word next to the correct number below.

| duck | frog | mouse | dog | cow | sheep | monkey | horse | bee | beetle | snake | spider |

1 _____	4 _____	7 _____	10 _____
2 _____	5 _____	8 _____	11 _____
3 _____	6 _____	9 _____	12 _____

b **T11.3** Listen and check. Practise saying the words.

c Put the animals into one of the groups below.

Animals with no legs   _____snake_____

Animals with two legs   _____ _____

Animals with four legs   _____ _____ _____ _____

_____ _____

Animals with more than four legs _____ _____ _____

Listen and read

9 **T11.4** Listen to and/or read about the animal world. Answer the questions.

a About how many animals species are there in the world? _ten million_

b How tall can an adult giraffe grow? _up to six metters_

c How long is the smallest mammal, Savi's pygmy shrew? _six centimeters_

d How much does a goliath frog weigh? _three K.m_

e How tall is an adult ostrich? _more than_

f How fast can a bee hummingbird move its wings? _20 to 50 times a second_

g How many types of kangaroo are there? _____

h How many bison were/are there in America in:
  i) the 1860s ⟶ _13 million Nort..._
  ii) the 1880s _few hundred_
  iii) now? _50,000 living in ..._

The animal world

We do not know how many species of animal there are, as people are discovering new ones all the time; but most scientists think that there are about ten million different animal species in the world.

Giraffes are the tallest animals on Earth. A large adult male giraffe can be up to 6 metres tall. Thanks to its long legs and neck, it can eat the leaves from the tops of trees.

The smallest animals are called protozoa, which have only one cell, and are so small that we cannot see them without a powerful microscope.

The smallest mammal is Savi's pygmy shrew – it is only 6 centimetres long, including its tail.

The goliath frog (*Rana Goliath*) of West Africa can be up to 75 centimetres long, and weighs about 3 kilograms. The goliath beetle is probably the world's largest beetle – it weighs more than 100 grams – about the same as two eggs.

The ostrich is the world's largest bird. An adult ostrich is more than 2.5 metres tall, but it cannot fly.

The bee hummingbird is probably the world's smallest bird – it is just 5 centimetres long and weighs less than 2 grams: it can stay still in the air by moving its wings twenty to fifty times a second. One of the largest birds which can fly is the South American condor: its wings are three metres from end to end.

There are more than fifty different types of kangaroo in Australia. When it is born, a baby kangaroo is less than 2.5 centimetres long: but an adult kangaroo can grow to more than 2 metres in height.

In the mid-1860s, there were about 13 million bison living in North America. By the mid-1880s, there were only a few hundred. Today there are about 50,000 bison in America, living in special parks.

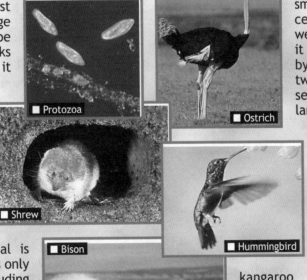

■ Protozoa
■ Shrew
■ Bison
■ Ostrich
■ Hummingbird

More about numbers

10 a Put the words into numbers.

1	sixty thousand	*60,000*
2	nineteen eighty-five	1985
3	three thousand	3000
4	ninety kilometres an hour	90 Km/h
5	nine point six	9.6
6	two hundred and fifty-three thousand	253,000
7	sixty-two million	62,000,000
8	two hundred and ninety-seven	297
9	two billion	2,000,000,000
10	nine hundred and sixty-three	963

b Put the numbers into words.

1	53,000	*fifty-three thousand*
2	150 km/h	one hundred fifty kilometres an hour.
3	3,000,000	three million.
4	8.5	eight point five.
5	348	three hundred fourty-eight.
6	2,000,000,000	Two billion and
7	5,600	Five thousand six hundred.
8	1980	ninty eighty and
9	350,000	three hundred fifty thousand
10	80,000,000	eightty Million.

Pronunciation
Numbers

11 a **T11.5** Listen to the pronunciation of these words. Practise saying them.

nine	nineteen	a hundred	a thousand
a million	a billion		

b **T11.6** Listen to the pronunciation of the numbers in Exercise 10a. Practise saying them.

c **T11.7** Practise saying the words in Exercise 10b. Then listen and check.

Articles

12 Complete these quiz questions with *a/an*, *the* or — (no word).

a How many players are there in __a__ baseball team?

b Where do _____ koala bears live?

c What is __the__ biggest desert in the world?

d What is __a__ ladybird?

e How many grams are there in ____a__ kilogram?

f How far is it from _the_ earth to _the_ moon?

g What languages do _____ Canadian's speak?

h What is _the_ capital of Colombia?

i How long does it take to boil __an__ egg?

j What's the name of _the_ river in London?

k Where was __the__ singer Kylie Minogue born?

l How fast can _the_ cheetahs run?

Improve your writing
Full stops, apostrophes and question marks

> **LOOK!**
>
> We use apostrophes:
>
> • in contracted forms:
>   *she's   can't   doesn't*
>
> • with possessive *'s*:
>   *John's friend   the world's favourite airline*
>
> We use full stops at the end of statements.
> *They're French.   I'm fine.*
>
> We use question marks at the end of questions.
> *Where do you live?   Where is it?*

13 Write apostrophes, full stops and question marks in the sentences below.

a Dogs can only see black and white: they can't see colours.

b I'm not sure what the answer is.

c Is it true that koala bears don't drink water?

d What is the world's largest animal?

e He doesn't know the answer.

f Where's the biggest lake in the world?

g What is Peter's pet dog's name?

Future plans
going to

Moumework

1 **a** Look at the pictures and write a sentence about what the people are going to do. Use the phrases in the box.

have lunch	~~have a baby~~	stop	get wet
buy a newspaper	paint the ceiling	go to bed	
play tennis			

1 She's _going to have a baby._

2 He_'s going to buy a newspaper._

3 They_'re going to play tennis._

4 The bus _____.

5 They_'re going to get wet._

6 He_'s going to bed._

7 They_'re paint the celeiling._

8 They _'re going to have lunch._

b **T12.1** Listen and check. Practise saying the sentences.

want to

2 Complete the sentences with the correct form of *want to*: positive, question or negative. Use the words in brackets.

a _Do you want to_ (you) rent a video this evening? There's nothing good on TV.

b I'm really not hungry. _I don't want to eat_ (I) eat anything, thank you.

c Valerie isn't going to look for a job when she leaves school. _She doesn't want to_ (she) go to university.

d _Does anybody want to_ (anybody) go for a cup of coffee when the lesson finishes?

e _Do your friends want to_ (your friends) go for a walk before we have dinner?

f Patricia is very tired. _She want to_ (she) go home and go to bed.

g _He doesn't want to_ (he) be a waiter, but it is the only job he can find.

h _Do you want to eat_ (you) anything to eat with your coffee?

Short answers

Short answers with *going to* and *want to*

Are you going to see her? **Yes, I am. No, we aren't.**

Does she want to come? **Yes, she does. No, she doesn't.**

3 Answer the questions about Neela, Enrico, Roman and Helena with short answers. Then answer the questions about yourself.

	Neela	Enrico	Roman and Helena
this weekend	have a haircut: Sat 10 am	play tennis: Sun 2 pm	relax
next week	go out with friends. Wed? Thurs?	go to the cinema on Wed	look at some cars and maybe buy one?
next year	go to college	have a holiday in Europe	get married

this weekend

a Is Neela going to have a haircut? _Yes, she is._

Are you going to have a haircut? _No, I'm not._

b Is Enrico going to play football? _No, he isn't._

Are you going to play football? _No, I'm not._

c Do Roman and Helena want to relax? _Yes, they do._

Do you want to relax? _No, I don't._

next week

d Does Neela want to study a lot? _No, she doesn't_

Do you want to study a lot? _Yes, I do._

e Is Enrico going to see a film? _Yes, he is_

Are you going to see a film? _No, aren't_

f Do Roman and Helena want to buy some clothes? _No, they don't_

Do you want to buy some clothes? _No, I don't_

next year

g Is Neela going to college? _Yes, she is_

Are you going to college? _Yes I are_

h Does Enrico want to have a holiday in Europe? _Yes, he does_

Do you want to have a holiday in Europe? _No, I don't_

i Are Roman and Helena going to get married? _Yes, they are_

Are you going to get married? _No, aren't_

would like to and want to

4 **a** Put the words in the correct order to make sentences with *would like to* or *want to*.

1 would like / a footballer / to be / when he's older / Stephen

Stephen would like to be a footballer when he's older.

2 you / something / like / to drink? / Would

Would you like somethin to drink? ?

3 and I / a table / near / My friends / the window, please / would like

My Friends and I would like a table, the window, Please
near

4 want / doesn't / stay / at home / to / Marc

Marc doesn't want to stay at home.

5 this evening? / to see / like / film / Which / would you

Which Film would you like to see this evening? ?

6 a / taxi / order / I'd / to / please / like

I'd like to order a taxi Please.

7 coffee, / We / thank you / any more / want / don't

We don't want any more coffee thank you.

8 in the park? / you / Would / like / for a walk / to go

Would you like to go for a walk in the Park?

b **T12.2** Listen and check. Practise saying the sentences.

Future forms

5 Correct the sentences. Add one extra word.

would

a Françoise/like to go to Japan one day.

'm

b Tomorrow's Saturday ... I going to stay in bed all day.

to

c Where do you want go?

like

d Would you to go out for lunch?

wants

e Chris isn't enjoying his holiday: he to go home!!

to

f My friends are going cook a special meal this evening.

to

g What would you like do tomorrow?

h We not going to have a holiday this year.

are

Word combinations

6 Write the words in the box in the correct category. Look at page 106 of the Students' Book, if necessary.

television	in bed
the shopping	the gym
a party	your homework
at home	the country
a meal	the cinema
a video	a barbecue
a shower	a concert
the housework	

a What can you **have**?
(four things)
a party
a barbecue
a meal
a shower

b Where can you **stay**?
(two places)
at home
in bed

c What can you **watch**?
(two things)
television
a video

d What can you **do**?
(three things)
the house work.
the shopping
your home work.

e What can you **go to**?
(four things)
the country
a concert
the cinema
the gym.

Suggestions and offers

7 **a** Mark, Barbara and their two children are on a camping holiday in the mountains. Complete the conversation with the words or phrases in the box.

shall	see	Let's	I'll	about	
idea	there's	like	don't	don't want	

MARK: Well, everybody ... what (1) ___shall___ we do today? Any ideas?

SUSIE: I'm not sure ... it depends on the weather. Is it sunny outside?

MARK: Just a minute ... no, not exactly ... in fact, it's raining again.

JAKE: Oh no! I (2) _____ another boring day like yesterday. Is there anything interesting we can go and see?

BARBARA: I know what we can do. (3) _____ have a look at the guide book. I'm sure we can find some ideas in there.

MARK: All right. Where is the guide book?

SUSIE: It's there, next to your feet.

MARK: Let's (4) _____ ... well, there's the Museum of Country Life; how (5) _____ that?

JAKE: Hmm ... is there anything more exciting?

MARK: Well, (6) _____ Aqua World. It's a Sea Life centre.

JAKE: Yes, that sounds better. Why (7) _____ we go there?

SUSIE: OK then, if you (8) _____ .

BARBARA: Shall I phone them to see what time it opens?

MARK: Good (9) _____ ! So everybody's happy, then.

          (10) _____ make some more coffee and then we can all get ready.

b **T12.3** Listen to the conversation and check your answers.

Pronunciation
I'll, we'll

8 **a** **T12.4** Listen to the pairs of sentences below. Notice the pronunciation of *'ll*.

1   I open the window.
    I'll open the window.

2   I turn on the heating.
    I'll turn on the heating.

3   We make lunch for you.
    We'll make lunch for you.

4   I phone for a taxi.
    I'll phone for a taxi.

5   I drive.
    I'll drive.

6   We buy some bread.
    We'll buy some bread.

b Listen again. Practise saying the sentences.

Prepositions

9 Complete the sentences with *in*, *on*, *to* or *at*.

a   Paul never goes out ___at___ the weekend.

b   Let's go _____ the cinema!

c   There's a party _____ John's house.

d   I'm so tired. I'm going to stay _____ bed all day tomorrow.

e   The weather can get really hot _____ summer.

f   I stayed _____ home all weekend.

g   We went _____ a rock concert on Saturday.

h   We went to the United States _____ holiday a few years ago.

Vocabulary booster

At the beach

10 a Label the picture with the words in the box.

a cliff   a cloud   a sandcastle   a surfer   a towel   a beach umbrella
a windsurfer   rocks   the beach   the sea   the sky   waves

1 _____

2 _____
  a cliff

3 _____

4 _____

5 _____

6 _____

7 _____

8 _____

9 _____
  the sea

10 _____

11 _____

12 _____

b **T12.5** Listen and check. Practise saying the words.

Future time expressions

11 **a** It is 9 am on Wednesday. Write the future time expressions in order.

tonight   this afternoon   next month   tomorrow evening next year   tomorrow morning next week   this weekend

9 am Wednesday

this afternoon

_____

_____

_____

_____

_____

_____

b It is now 4 pm on Friday, April 8th 2005. What's another way to say ...

1 10 am, Saturday 9th April?

   tomorrow morning

2 9 pm, Saturday?

   _____

3 The week 11–17th April?

   _____

4 Saturday and Sunday, 9th and 10th April?

   _____

5 May 2005?

   _____

6 2006?

   _____

7 10 pm Friday 8th April?

   _____

Listen and read

12 [T12.6] Listen to and/or read the world weather report for the week ending 15th March. Complete the information in the table.

	What was the weather like?	Extra information
Chicago	snow, windy	
San Francisco	_____	
Queensland	_____	475 mm of rain in five days
Jerez de la Frontera	_____	_____
The Balkans	_____	
North-east Italy	_____	_____
Irkutsk	_____	_____

The World Weather Report

March 15th

There was heavy snow and windy weather in Chicago on Monday, and there was also heavy rain on the west coast of the United States – particularly in and around the city of San Francisco.

Things were no better on the other side of the world in Australia – there was extremely heavy rain in the state of Queensland, with 475 mm of rain falling in just five days.

In south-west Europe, there was more hot, sunny weather with the town of Jerez de la Frontera in the south of Spain the hottest place. The temperature was 30 degrees, the warmest so far this year.

It wasn't all good news in Europe, however. There was heavy snow in the Balkans, and parts of north-eastern Italy on Monday and Tuesday. Things are getting a little better in the city of Irkutsk, in eastern Siberia, however: the temperature went above zero degrees for the first time since last November.

Vocabulary
The weather

13 Read the sentences and describe the weather.

a   You're going to need your umbrellas if you go out.
It's raining. /It's wet.

b   Can you pass me my sunglasses ... that's better. Now I can see!!
_____

c   Thirty-five degrees!! Let's go for a swim!
_____

d   Please drive carefully: in some places you can't see more than five metres.
_____

e   What a beautiful spring day. Let's go for a walk!
_____

f   The weather's not too bad today: there's no sun, but it isn't raining.
_____

g   Look outside! The garden is completely white!!
_____

h   Put on your warm clothes if you go out!
_____

i   All the leaves are falling off the trees!!
_____

Talking about the weather

14 a Match the two parts of these mini-conversations about the weather.

1   It's raining. Have you got your umbrella?   d
2   Did you hear the weather forecast?   ☐
3   It's a lovely day, isn't it?   ☐
4   It's very foggy outside.   ☐
5   What's the weather like?   ☐
6   Did you have a good holiday? Was the weather OK?   ☐

a   Yes, beautiful.
b   It's going to be cold tomorrow, but warmer at the weekend.
c   It's snowing! Can we go out?
d   No. Can I borrow one?
e   Great, thanks. And we were lucky with the weather. It was hot most days and it only rained once.
f   Yes. I'll drive slowly.

b   **T12.7**   Listen and check your answers. Practise saying the conversations.

Improve your writing
Write about a holiday place

15 a Make notes about a popular holiday place in your country under these headings.

- Where it is
- The most important attractions
- Places to eat and drink
- Things to do for children
- Excursions

b   Write a paragraph about the place using some of the phrases in the box.

> ... is in the north/south/east/
> west of ...
> It's one of the (oldest/most
> beautiful) towns in ...
> It has a large number of ...
> The best ... is ... which has ...
> There are lots of places to ...
> You can enjoy ...
> For children there is ...
> You can also visit ...

Vocabulary

Education and learning

1 Look at the extracts from some textbooks. What subjects are they about?

Science   Law   Economics   ~~Business Studies~~
Geography   Information Technology   Medicine
Engineering   Politics   Design   History
Mathematics   Literature

A   Business Studies

A business which puts all its money into the stock market can easily lose everything. For example, in the crash of 1987

B   _____

São Paulo, Brazil, is South America's largest city and one of the fastest-growing cities in the world. It is the commercial centre of

C   _____

The memory of a computer consists of microchips. There are two types: ROM (read-only memory) contains permanent instructions,

D   _____

In the fourteenth century, Arab traders sailed across the Indian Ocean and introduced Islam to many Asian countries. In 1511,

E   _____

Romeo and Juliet was one of Shakespeare's early plays but in it he wrote some of his most beautiful poetry. When Romeo leaves

F   _____

It is often better for the person not to take antibiotics if the illness isn't serious. In the past doctors often gave too many antibiotics and

G   _____

H_2O – This chemical symbol for water means that each water molecule contains two atoms of hydrogen and one atom of

H   _____

$875 \div 43 = 20.3488$

I   _____

The world's longest bridges are now all suspension bridges.

J   _____

In the case of Walker versus Thompson, where a man killed his business partner, the judge gave him 20 years in prison because

K   _____

Bauhaus furniture and ordinary objects were famous in the early twentieth century but are still very popular today. For example, Bauhaus chairs and lamps

L   _____

The Communist Party was started by Vladimir Ilich Lenin in 1903. Communism became popular, first in Russia and later in China

M   _____

The economy of a country depends in part on its natural resources. For example, if a country is rich in diamonds, or oil,

2 Choose the best alternatives in the text.

Is there really a big difference between boys and girls at school? New research says there is.

When British girls between the ages of five and eleven go to (a) *primary* / *secondary* school, they often do better at school than boys. But now older girls are doing better at (b) *primary* / *secondary* school too.

Many people think that boys (c) *make* / *get* better grades in science and mathematics and girls do well in languages and art. But more and more women apply (d) *to* / *for* courses in law and engineering at university and many (e) *do* / *make* courses in mathematics and economics.

Every year, tens of thousands of British teenagers (f) *take* / *pass* their 'A' or 'Advanced' level exams. Young people need to (g) *pass* / *succeed* these exams if they want to go to university. But in 2005, more boys than girls (h) *passed* / *failed* their 'A' levels. Too many young boys leave school without (i) *doing* / *getting* qualifications. They then (j) *choose* / *do* careers in badly paid jobs.

Infinitive of purpose

3 Last Friday, Carol went into town. Why did she visit these places? Write sentences with the infinitive of purpose, using the phrases in the box.

| borrow some books   have lunch   buy some meat |
| ~~get some money~~   buy some fruit |
| catch the bus home   visit her sick friend |
| send a parcel to her cousin |

a   the bank

She went to the bank to get some money.

b   the library

_____

_____

c   the post office

_____

_____

d   the hospital

_____

_____

e   the greengrocer's

_____

_____

f   the butcher's

_____

_____

g   the bus station

_____

_____

h   The Oak Tree Café

_____

_____

Infinitives with and without *to*

4 Choose the correct form in the sentences below.

a   Taka wants *learn* / *to learn* more about computers.

b   Paul is studying English *get* / *to get* a better job.

c   It might *be* / *to be* better if you do it yourself.

d   I'm going to the supermarket *buy* / *to buy* some bread. Do you want anything?

e   Charles probably won't *pass* / *to pass* the exam.

f   Thousands of people went to Greece *to watch* / *watch* the Olympics.

g   We might not *have* / *to have* a holiday this year.

Listen and read

5 **T13.1** Listen to and/or read about *The five ages of English*.
Match the pictures with the paragraphs.

A ___3___

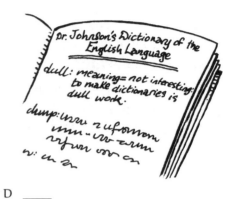

D ___

B ___

C ___

E ___

The five ages of English

1 Old English
From about the ninth century, the Vikings – who lived in what is now Sweden and Norway, began to arrive in the north of England. The language people spoke began to change. In the south of England, people began to translate books from Latin into English.

2 Middle English
In 1066, the Normans invaded England and French became the official language. Most educated people had to speak three languages: French, Latin and English! At this time, English literature began to develop. One of the most famous writers was the poet Geoffrey Chaucer in the fourteenth century. His language is a little like the English of today.

3 Early Modern English
(1450–1750)
This period includes the time of William Shakespeare – England's greatest writer. By the end of the seventeenth century, great scientists, like Isaac Newton, wrote in English, not in Latin. The British Empire began, and the English language travelled across the Atlantic to North America, and across Asia to India.

4 Modern English
(1750–1950)
English was now a national language. The first dictionary – Johnson's Dictionary – appeared in 1755, and the first grammar books appeared soon after. As the British Empire grew in the nineteenth century, English became a more international language. People began to learn English around the world. The first English language textbooks appeared in the 1930s.

5 Late Modern English
(from 1950)
Now, English language teaching is an important international industry. After World War II, the United States became the most important economic and cultural power in the world, and a world market in audio-visual communication began. CNN International began in 1989 and the Internet developed in the 1990s. English became a global language, with about two billion speakers.

Vocabulary booster
In an Internet café

6 **a** Match the things in the picture to the words in the box.

screen	☐
printer	☐
chair	☑1
keyboard	☐
mouse	☐
CD-ROM drive	☐
document	☐
desk	☐
modem	☐
scanner	☐

b **T13.2** Listen and check. Practise saying the words.

might and *might not*

7 **a** Rewrite the sentences using *might* or *might not* instead of the words in bold.

1 **Perhaps** we'll go swimming this afternoon.
We _might go swimming this afternoon._

2 **It's possible that** the plane **will** arrive late.
The plane _____ .

3 **Maybe** you'll be rich one day, if you work hard.
You _____ .

4 **It's possible that I won't** be able to come next week.
I _____ .

5 I **possibly won't** see Frank this weekend.
I _____ .

6 **Perhaps** Philip **won't** stay until the end of the course.
Philip _____ .

7 The government **will possibly** change soon.
The government _____ .

8 **Maybe** the exam **won't** be as difficult as you think.
The exam _____ .

b **T13.3** Listen to the sentences. Practise saying them.

will and *won't* (*probably*)

8 **a** Rearrange the words to make sentences.

1 probably / a / be / It / tomorrow / will / nice day
It will probably be a nice day tomorrow.

2 time / won't / There / to stop for lunch / be / probably

_____

3 be / will / class / probably / for / late / Martha

_____

4 need / your / You / probably / umbrella / won't

_____

5 be able / tomorrow / I / to come / won't / probably

_____

6 soon / There / probably / be / an election / will

_____

b **T13.4** Listen to the sentences. Practise saying them.

might (not), *will* and *won't*

9 **a** Tom, Meg, and Sampath are three school friends who have just finished their exams. Read the notes about their plans for the future.

Meg

Tom

Sampath

> **LOOK!**
>
> We use *will* / *might* / *might not* / *won't* to talk about possibility.
>
> *They might get married.*
> *I'll probably go to university.*
>
> We use *going to* to talk about **intentions**.
>
> *I'm going to do a business course.*

	Holiday?	University?	Job?
Tom	no plans – Greece maybe	maybe not!	my father's company, probably
Meg	probably Spain with my parents	next year, probably	all my family are doctors, so why not me?
Sampath	don't think I'll have time	not sure – perhaps get a job abroad instead	who knows – an actor?

b Use the information to write sentences with *might*, *might not*, *will probably* or *probably won't*.

1 Tom *might go to Greece for his holiday.*_____ (go to Greece)

2 Meg _____ . (go to Spain)

3 Sampath _____ . (have time for a holiday)

4 Tom _____ . (go to university)

5 Meg _____ . (go to university next year)

6 Sampath _____ . (get a job abroad instead)

7 Tom _____ . (work for his father's company)

8 Meg _____ . (become a doctor)

9 Sampath _____ . (become an actor)

10 Complete these sentences so that they are true for you.

a I _*'m going to*___ study in Australia next year.

b I _*probably won't*_ get good marks in my English test.

c I _____ do an IT course this year.

d I _____ take an English exam soon.

e I _____ apply for a new job this year.

f I _____ earn a lot of money next year.

g I _____ study in the USA this year.

h I _____ read a book in English this week.

Pronunciation
Contracted forms

11 **a** ⬛ **T13.5** Listen to the sounds and the example words below.

/ɑː/	art	father	car
/əʊ/	know	go	home
/ɜː/	work	girl	birth

b ⬛ **T13.6** Notice the same sounds in these contracted forms.

/ɑː/	aren't	can't
/əʊ/	don't	won't
/ɜː/	weren't	

Improve your writing
Abbreviations on application forms (*Mr*, *Mrs*, *Dr*, *n/a*)

12

a Write the abbreviations for these words.

1   Mister   _____

2   January   _____

3   Doctor   _____

4   October   _____

5   not applicable   _____

6   December   _____

7   Number   _____

8   September   _____

9   *et cetera* (= and the others)   _____

b Here are some other abbreviations you see on application forms. Match the words on the right to the correct abbreviations.

1   Ave   Street

2   e.g.   Avenue

3   kg   kilometres

4   km   North, South, East, West

5   Mon/Tues/Wed/Thurs   *exempli gratia* (= for example)

6   N/S/E/W   Park

7   Pk   Road

8   Rd   kilograms

9   St   United States of America

10 tel   United Kingdom

11 UK   telephone

12 USA   Monday, Tuesday, Wednesday, Thursday

c Rewrite the following with abbreviations.

1   Mister James Hewson
    Mr James Hewson _____
    _____

2   2 kilograms
    _____
    _____

3   63 Stamford Street
    _____
    _____

4   irregular verbs, for example bring and buy
    _____
    _____

5   Queen's Park Road
    _____
    _____

6   London South-West 7
    _____
    _____

7   10 kilometres
    _____
    _____

8   arrived in the United Kingdom from the United States
    _____
    _____

9   telephone number: 020 7939 3671
    _____
    _____

10 classes are on Tuesday and Thursday
    _____
    _____

11 January–March and April–September
    _____
    _____

Vocabulary
Ways of communicating

1 What are these instructions for? Choose one of the phrases from the box.

---

leaving a phone message	receiving a text message
sending an e-mail	making a phone call
taking a photo	going on the Internet
sending something by post	paying by phone
sending a card	writing a letter
sending a faxc	

---

a After you hear a BEEP, speak slowly and clearly. Don't forget to say your name ...

leaving a phone message

b Write your address and the date in the top right hand corner. Start with Dear and the name of the ...

c When you've finished writing, click on the Send button at the top of the screen.

d Put the document into the machine ... then dial the number and press the button that ...

e Press the ON button and then use the zoom to make the picture bigger or smaller. Then press the button on the top ...

f ... if you can't find the information you want, click on the Links and you'll see a list of other websites.

g Press the green button, and you'll hear a tone ... then dial the phone number. Don't forget the code.

h Don't forget to write your name inside! Then put it in an envelope, write the address and post it.

i Go to the post office and they will weigh your parcel and tell you how much it costs. Buy stamps and then leave it at the post office.

j You hear a beep on your phone and it says 'new message'. Then you open the in-box and the message appears.

k You need to give your credit card number over the phone and also your address.

Irregular past participles

2 a Find the past participles of the verbs. What is the mystery word?

1	sleep
2	make
3	lose
4	stand
5	speak
6	take
7	drive
8	write
9	say
10	come
11	give
12	keep
13	tell
14	become
15	see

1 S L E P T

b T14.1 Listen and check. Practise saying the verbs.

Present Perfect

3 Complete the sentences with the Present Perfect form of the verbs in brackets.

a Martin __has sent__ (send) hundreds of e-mails to his favourite singer, Kyla.

b Mark and Yumiko _____ (see) all of Kurosawa's films.

c Oh no! I _____ (leave) the tickets at home!

d Terry Guy _____ (write) more than twenty books.

e Wei tzu _____ (lose) her keys six times this year!

f I _____ (never read) any Shakespeare plays, but I'd like to!

g I'm sorry but I _____ (forget) your name.

h We _____ (check) our computer but we cannot find your name.

i I _____ (buy) a present for Connie – it's her birthday tomorrow.

j Tricia _____ (never have) a bicycle.

Positive and negative

4 **a** The first Women's Soccer World Cup was in China in 1991. There have been two more World Cups: here are the winners and the losing finalists.

Year	Venue	Winners	Goals	Losing finalists	Goals
1991	China	United States	2	Norway	1
1995	Sweden	Norway	2	Germany	0
1999	USA	United States (United States won on penalties)	0	China	0
2003	USA	Germany	2	Sweden	1

b Complete the sentences with the Present perfect of the verb.

1 There __have been__ (be) three World Cups up to now.

2 The United States _____ (win) the competition twice.

3 They _____ (not have) the competition in South America.

4 Germany _____ (play) in one World Cup Final.

5 The United States _____ (never lose) in the Final.

6 There _____ (be) one World Cup in Europe.

7 Norway and the United States _____ (play) in two finals.

8 Germany _____ (not win) the World Cup.

9 Norway _____ (score) three goals in the World Cup Finals.

10 There _____ (be) one final which finished in a penalty competition.

Questions and short answers

> **Short answers with the Present perfect**
>
> LOOK!
>
> **Have** you/I/we/they **done it?**
>   **Yes,** I/you/we/they **have.**
>   **No,** I/you/we/they **haven't.**
>
> **Has** he/she/it **done it?**
>   **Yes,** he/she/it **has.**
>   **No,** he/she/it **hasn't.**

5 **a** Read about the people below. Then complete the questions and write the correct short answer.

Richard Marshall and his wife Elaine are retired. Recently they moved to a new house in Hexham, a town near Newcastle, in the north of England. Richard was born in Hexham, but Elaine is originally from Aberdeen, a town in the north of Scotland.

Gordon Marshall – Richard and Elaine's son – was born in Newcastle but he now lives with his wife and daughter in Leeds, a town about 150 km away, where he is a teacher. He's also worked abroad: he worked in a restaurant in France when he was younger.

Sarah Marshall – Gordon's wife – has always wanted her own business. Her daughter Rebecca left school last year, and now they're in business together. She and her mother have opened a new sandwich shop called *Crusts* in Leeds city centre. It's the first time they've worked together!

1   __Has__   Richard always lived in Hexham?
    __Yes, he has.__

2 _____ Elaine ever lived in another town?
   _____

3 _____ they always lived in the same house?
   _____

4 _____ Gordon always been a teacher?
   _____

5 _____ he ever worked abroad?
   _____

6 _____ Gordon and Sarah always lived in Leeds?
   _____

7 _____ Sarah had her own business before?
   _____

8 _____ Rebecca left school?
   _____

b **T14.2** Listen and check. Practise saying the questions and short answers.

Pronunciation
Past participles

6 **a** Look at the list of past participles below. Underline the sound which has a different pronunciation.

1	sent	met	made	said	read
2	done	gone	run	won	begun
3	made	played	stayed	paid	fed
4	stolen	spoken	told	got	chosen
5	caught	bought	drawn	shown	taught

b **T14.3** Listen to the pronunciation of the words on the recording. Practise saying them.

Spelling
Regular past participles

> **LOOK!**
>
> To form the past participle of regular verbs we add *-ed*:
> play ➡ play**ed**
>
> If the regular verb ends in *-e* we add *-d* only:
> decide ➡ decid**ed**
>
> say and pay take *-aid*:
> say ➡ s**aid**
> pay ➡ p**aid**
>
> Verbs ending in consonant + *-y* change the *-y* to *-ied*:
> study ➡ stud**ied**
> try ➡ tr**ied**
>
> Verbs ending in consonant + vowel + consonant, double the consonant:
> study ➡ stud**ied**
> plan ➡ plan**ned**

7 Look at the sentences below. Is the spelling of the past participle correct or not? If it is incorrect, write the correct spelling.

a Have you ever **staid** in an expensive hotel? ✗

  ___stayed___

b Have you **used** this kind of computer before?

  _____

c I've never **tryed** Japanese tea before.

  _____

d We haven't **decided** where to go on holiday.

  _____

e My mother has always **studyed** music.

  _____

f I have never **stopped** loving you.

  _____

g Exams have never **worried** me.

  _____

h Have you ever **plaid** baseball?

  _____

i I've **livd** in this apartment all my life.

  _____

j My cousin has **traveled** all over the world.

  _____

Time words with the Present perfect

8 Complete the sentences with the time words in the box.

never	just	already	ever	recently	~~before~~
always					

a I don't know what this is: I haven't eaten it

  ___before___ .

b Have you _____ met anyone famous?

c Has anyone seen any good films _____ ?

d I've _____ seen Titanic so I don't want to see it again.

e I've _____ liked pop music; I prefer jazz.

f Laura has _____ wanted to be a musician. She loves playing music.

g A: Would you like a cake?

  B: No thanks, I've _____ eaten.

Word order

9 Put the sentences into the correct order.

a 's – Maria – baby – had – a !

  ___Maria's had a baby!___

b just – married – They – got – 've

  _____

c bought – Dubai – flat – 've – in – recently – We – a

  _____

d never – tram – father – on – been – 's – My – a – before

  _____

  _____

e studied – already – Stefanie – perfect – the – 's – present

  _____

  _____

f you – outside – Have – slept – ever?

  _____

Time words with the Present perfect and Past simple

10 a Complete the mini-conversations with the correct form of the verbs in brackets: Present perfect or Past simple.

1

A: Fantastic! I (a) __'ve just passed__ (just pass) my exam.

B: Oh well done!

2

A: How's Ana? I (b) _____ (not see) her recently

B: I (c) _____ (speak) to her yesterday. She's very well.

3

A: I'm going to Paris next week. (d) _____ _____ (you ever go) there?

B: Yes. We (e) _____ (go) there about two years ago.

A: (f) _____ (you like) it?

B: It (g) _____ (be) great!

4

A: (h) _____ (you ever sell) anything on the Internet?

B: No, I (i) _____ . What about you?

A: Last year I (j) _____ (try) to sell my car but no one (k) _____ (buy) it.

5

A: Can we have the bill, please?

B: Don't worry. I (l) _____ (already pay) it.

A: Thanks very much!

b **T14.4** Listen and check your answers. Practise saying the conversations.

Real life
Telephoning

11 Put the words in the box in the correct place in the conversations.

can	here	'd	are	this	to	's	'll	a
this	to	that						

a   A: Hello, can I speak ~~to~~ Greg please?

b   B: I'm sorry, he's not at the moment.

c   A: Can you ask him phone me, please?

d   B: OK … What your number?

A: 732 9302.

e   A: Hello, SA International, I help you?

f   B: I like to speak to Mr Cornwell, please

g   A: One moment I connect you.

B: Hello

h   A: Is Jim Cornwell

B: Speaking.

i   A: Hello, is Susan Heyman from Business Solutions

j   B: Oh hi, Susan. How you?

k   A: Hello, is Matthew speaking. I'm not here at the

l   moment. Please leave message after the tone.

Vocabulary booster
The post

12 **a** Match the pictures to the words in the box.

postcard	☐
birthday card	☐
post box	☐
parcel	☐
envelope	☐
invitation	1
stamps	☐
note	☐
postman	☐
posting a letter	☐

b **T14.5** Listen and check. Practise saying the words.

Improve your writing
Writing a note

13 **a** Read the note below and answer these questions.

1 Who is it for? _____Joe_____
2 Who wrote it? _____
3 Where did she go? _____
4 When will she be back? _____

> Hi Joe
> Hope you had a good day at work!
> Gone to supermarket to get
> something for dinner. Back at 6.
> See you then.
> Love
>   Fiona

> **LOOK!**
> When we write a note, we often miss out words like:
> - articles   ~~the~~ supermarket
> - pronouns and auxiliary verbs   ~~I~~ hope ...
>   ~~I've~~ gone
> - and we use shorter forms   6 = 6 o'clock
>   Hi!
>   Thanks = Thank you

b Tom is on holiday. Charlotte is looking after his cats. Cross out or change the underlined words to make Tom's note for Charlotte

>   Hi
> ~~Good morning~~ Charlotte!
> <u>Thank you very much</u> for feeding <u>the</u> cats!!
> <u>There are some</u> tins of cat food in <u>the</u> cupboard
> next to <u>the</u> window.
> Please give <u>them</u> one tin ONLY!! <u>I'll</u> see you on
> Saturday, about 1 <u>o'clock</u>.
> Love
>   Tom

Vocabulary
Town facilities

1 Here is a list of places that Ali wants to visit while he is in Branton. Use the list to answer the questions.

Where can he …

a   sit with a coffee and watch people walk past?   _the square_

b   see paintings?   _____

c   watch an athletics meeting?   _____

d   go shopping?   _____

e   see interesting old objects and learn about history?   _____

f   sunbathe and go swimming?   _____

g   sit and relax in a place with grass and trees?   _____

h   go on a boat trip?   _____

i   go to pray?   _____

j   visit a place where kings lived in the past?   _____

the park

the art gallery

the beach

the ~~square~~

the sports stadium

the canal

the palace

the museum

the shopping centre

the mosque

2

Which A is a place where aeroplanes take off and land?	A I R P O R T
Which B goes across a road, railway line or a river?	B _ _ _ _ _ _
Which C is a large strong building?	C _ _ _ _ _ _
Which D is something you ask for when you're lost?	D _ _ _ _ _ _ _ _ _
Which E is the opposite of *beginning*?	E _ _
Which F means *wonderful* or *great*?	F _ _ _ _ _ _ _ _
Which G is a place where you see paintings?	G _ _ _ _ _ _
Which H is a small mountain?	H _ _ _
Which I is the opposite of *boring*?	I _ _ _ _ _ _ _ _ _ _
Which J is a trip from one place to another?	J _ _ _ _ _ _
Which K is 1,000 metres?	K _ _ _ _ _ _ _ _ _
Which M is a very high place – the Matterhorn, for example?	M _ _ _ _ _ _ _
When something is N, it means that you have to do it.	N _ _ _ _ _ _ _ _
Which O is the opposite of *closed*?	O _ _ _
Which P is a place in a town with trees, grass, flowers etc.?	P _ _ _
Which R is the Thames, the Amazon and the Nile?	R _ _ _ _ _
Which S is a stone model of a famous person?	S _ _ _ _ _ _
Which T is something you have to buy when you travel by bus/train etc.?	T _ _ _ _ _
Which U is the opposite of *over*?	U _ _ _ _
Which W is a way to get from one place to another using your legs?	W _ _ _

Prepositions of movement

3 Choose the correct preposition.

a Walk (along) / into / out of the main street until you come to the main square.

b If you want to get to the main shopping area, go *into / over / through* the river to the north of the city.

c It's a long walk *from / out of / up* the hill, but at the end of it you can see the whole city ... it's wonderful!

d There's a bus stop near the school where you can get a bus *down / over / to* the town centre.

e The Number Six tram goes *across / past / through* the door of our apartment.

f You can now fly *across / along / past* the Atlantic Ocean in less than six hours.

g How long does it take to drive *down / from / to* here to the coast?

h Most visitors park their cars outside and then walk *along / into / over* the centre.

4 Complete the letter with the words in the box.

over	past	~~to~~	down	from	across
along	out of				

Dear Susie,

Here are instructions to get (a) __to__ my house (b) _____ the railway station:

You get off the train and walk (c) _____ the bridge to the station entrance. Come (d) _____ the station and walk (e) _____ the steps. You can see lots of taxis and a car park there. Walk (f) _____ the car park and you come to a big road. Turn left and walk (g) _____ the road for about ten minutes (h) _____ some shops. My flat is in a big white building on the right, called Redford Mansions.

See you tomorrow,

Jane

have to, don't have to

5 Bruce, George, Alizia and Meera all work for GONE!! airline. Complete the sentences about them with *has/have to* or *doesn't/don't have to*.

Bruce is a member of the cabin crew.

a He __has to__ look after passengers.

b He _____ use a computer.

c He _____ look smart.

George is a pilot.

d He _____ fly the plane.

e He _____ serve food.

f He _____ wear a uniform.

Alizia and Meera work at the GONE!! Call Centre near London.

g They _____ wear a uniform.

h They _____ travel a lot.

Questions and short answers

6 **a** Write questions as in the exampleThen write the short answer.

> **LOOK!**
>
> **Short answers with *have to***
>
> **Do** I/you/we/they **have to** go?
> **Yes,** I/you/we/they **do**.
> **No,** I/you/we/they **don't**.
>
> **Does** he/she/it **have to** go?
> **Yes,** he/she/it **does**.
> **No,** he/she/it **doesn't**.

1   Bruce / have to / look after the passengers?
    Does Bruce have to look after the passengers?
    Yes, he does.

2   he / have to / use a computer?
    _____ ?
    _____

3   he / have to / look smart?
    _____ ?
    _____

4   George / have to / fly the plane?
    _____ ?
    _____

5   he / have to / serve food?
    _____ ?
    _____

6   he / have to / wear a uniform?
    _____ ?
    _____

7   Alizia and Meera / have to / wear a uniform?
    _____ ?
    _____

8   they / have to / travel a lot?
    _____ ?
    _____

b **T15.1** Listen to the sentences. Practise saying them.

have to, don't have to, can, can't

7 **a** Look at the information about flights to New York on two airlines – BAC and **GONE**!! and complete the sentences with *have to*, *don't have to*, *can* or *can't*.

	BAC	GONE!!
Ticket price	1st class return ticket: £1,500	Standby ticket: £150
Check-in time	be at the airport 1 hour before	3 hours before
Before the flight	special VIP lounge	wait in Departure Lounge only
Food and drink	yes – free	buy sandwiches and drinks on plane
In-flight film	yes	no
Seats	seat numbers	no seat numbers
Duty-free goods	yes	no

On BAC airlines:

1   You ___*have to*___ check in one hour before.
2   You _____ wait in the VIP lounge.
3   You _____ pay for your food and drinks.
4   You _____ watch an in-flight film.
5   You _____ sit in a particular seat.
6   You _____ buy duty-free goods.

On GONE!! airlines:

7   You _____ arrive at the airport three hours before.
8   You _____ use the VIP lounge.
9   You _____ pay for your food and drinks.
10 You _____ watch an in-flight film.
11 You _____ sit where you want.
12 You _____ buy duty-free goods.

b **T15.2** Listen to the sentences. Practise saying them.

Listen and read
Unusual places to visit

8 **T15.3** Listen and/or read about three unusual places to visit, and complete the table.

	Blue Lagoon	London Bridge	Guggenheim Museums
What it is	_____ _____	_____ _____	_____ _____
Where it is	*45 km from* *Reykjavik, Iceland*	_____ _____	_____ _____
Why people go there	_____ _____	_____ _____	_____ _____

Blue Lagoon – Iceland

Iceland – a country in the North Atlantic near the Arctic Circle – probably isn't the first place you think of for a perfect beach holiday. But every year, thousands of people take off their clothes and swim at the Blue Lagoon, a beach near the Arctic Circle and just 45 km from the capital city, Reykjavik. The air temperature can be as low as minus10 degrees: but the water comes from underground and is naturally hot – the usual water temperature is between 35 and 40 degrees. It's like taking a hot bath in the open air!!

London Bridge – USA!!

The original London Bridge actually isn't in London at all ... and it doesn't even pass over a river!! American businessman Robert P McCulloch bought the bridge for $2.5 million in 1968 and moved it – stone by stone – across the Atlantic Ocean. He rebuilt it in Lake Havasu City, Arizona – a small town in the middle of the desert, where the temperature is often more than 40 degrees. Nowadays, thousands of tourists come to see the bridge, and there is an English village with watersports facilities, shops and restaurants.

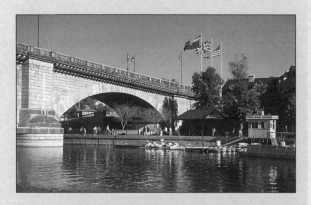

The Guggenheim Museums

There are not one but five Guggenheim Museums. Solomon R Guggenheim opened the first collection of modern art in New York in 1959. Another museum opened in Italy, and then, in 1997, two more Guggenheims opened: one in Berlin and the other in the Basque city of Bilbao, in the north-west of Spain.
It is now one of Spain's biggest tourist attractions, and every year hundreds of thousands of people come to see the paintings and other works of art. The newest Guggenheim museum is the Virtual Museum – the world's biggest Internet art gallery.

Real life
Following directions

9 **a** Find where you are on the map. Then find the National Gallery of Scotland. Complete the directions to the Scottish National Gallery, using the words in the box.

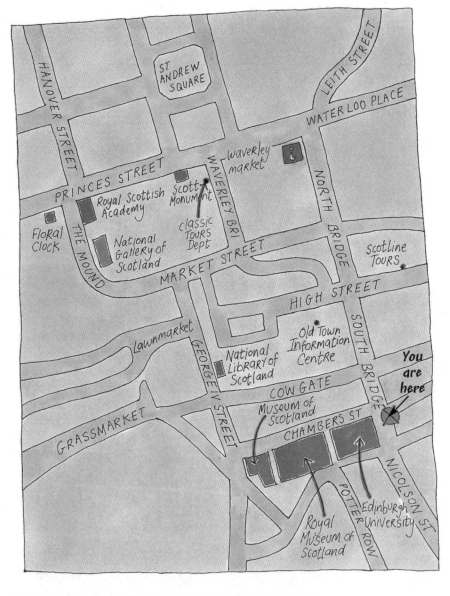

b T15.4 Listen and check your answers. Practise saying the directions at the same time as the recording.

c You are at the National Gallery. Complete the directions to the Museum of Scotland.

Come (1) __out__ of the National Gallery and (2) _____ left.
(3) _____ the first turning
(4) _____ the right and
(5) _____ straight on,
(6) _____ the National Library of Scotland. (7) _____ you come to Chambers Street, turn
(8) _____ and the Royal Museum is (9) _____ the
(10) _____ .

d T15.5 Listen and check your answers. Practise saying the directions at the same time as the recording.

| turn | the | on | past | _along_ | straight | on |

Go (1) __along__ South Bridge Road. Go (2) _____ on for about 500 metres until the end of the road. When you come to Princes Street
(3) _____ left. Go straight (4) _____ for about 500 metres,
(5) _____ the market and the Scott Monument, and take the second street on (6) _____ left. It's called The Mound. The gallery is
(7) _____ the left.

Vocabulary booster
A shopping centre

10 **a** Label the pictures with words from the box.

> an escalator   a push chair   steps   shoppers   a clothes shop
> a department store   a shop window   automatic doors   ~~a lift~~   a bench

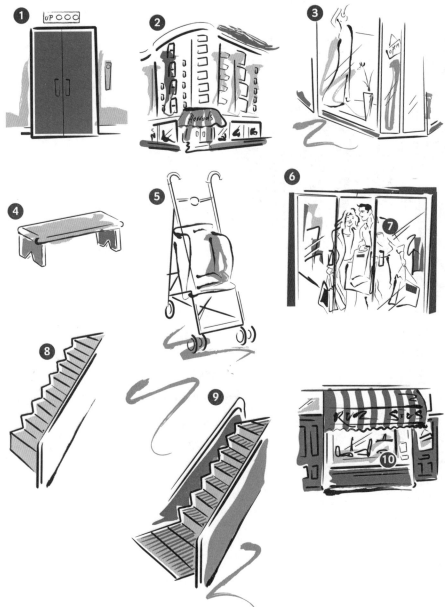

1 *a lift*
2 _____
3 _____
4 _____
5 _____

6 _____
7 _____
8 _____
9 _____
10 _____

b **T15.6** Listen to the pronunciation of the words. Practise saying them.

Vocabulary
Adjectives to describe towns

11 Write the missing letters to make adjectives to describe towns.

a f u n

b f _ s h _ _ n _ b _ _

c a t _ _ _ _ t _ v _

d l _ v _ _ y

e t r _ d _ _ _ _ n _ _

f p _ _ c _ _ _ l

g i n t _ _ _ s _ _ _ g

h e x _ _ n _ _ v _

i f r _ _ _ d _ y

j m _ d _ _ n

Spelling and pronunciation
Silent letters

12 **a** All the words below have at least one silent letter. Which letter(s) don't we pronounce? Cross out the silent letters, as in the example.

1 cas~~t~~le   7 design
2 straight   8 know
3 scenery   9 sights
4 highest   10 right
5 building   11 sign
6 through   12 listen

b **T15.7** Listen to the pronunciation of the words. Practise saying them.

Improve your writing
A postcard

13 **a** James and Thelma are spending a few days in London. They have written a postcard to their neighbours in the United States. Read the postcard and write the words from the box into the correct space.

Hi	nearest	have	great
English	seen	Bye	tea	in

(1) __Hi__ everybody!!
Here we are (2) ____ London!
The weather isn't too bad and we're
having a (3) ____ time. We've
(4) ____ the Changing of the Guard at
Buckingham Palace, and right now
we're having a cup of (5) ____ .
The kids want to go to the (6) ____
McDonald's, but Thelma and I want to
(7) ____ lunch in a real old
(8) ____ pub near Westminster Abbey.
(9) ____ for now!
Bob, Thelma and the kids

The Watts Family
5831 Hills Avenue
Daytoun,
Virginia VA 838
USA

b Choose a place and write a postcard to someone you know. Use some of the phrases below.

Useful language		
Here we are in ...	We've seen ...	The weather is(n't) ...
Right now, we're ...	We want to ...	We're having a ...time
We're going to ...	... want(s) to go to ...	Bye for now!

PRONUNCIATION TABLE

Consonants		Vowels	
Symbol	Key Word	Symbol	Key Word
p	**p**et	iː	sl**ee**p
b	**b**oat	ɪ	b**i**t
t	**t**op	e	b**e**d
d	**d**o	æ	c**a**t
k	**c**at	ɑː	f**a**ther
g	**g**olf	ɒ	cl**o**ck
tʃ	**ch**ur**ch**	ɔː	b**ough**t
dʒ	**j**eans	ʊ	b**oo**k
f	**f**ew	uː	b**oo**t
v	**v**iew	ʌ	b**u**t
θ	**th**irsty	ɜː	b**i**rd
ð	**th**ough	ə	broth**er**
s	**s**it	eɪ	d**ay**
z	**z**oo	əʊ	ph**o**ne
ʃ	fre**sh**	aɪ	b**y**
ʒ	lei**s**ure	aʊ	n**ow**
h	**h**at	ɔɪ	b**oy**
m	**m**other	ɪə	d**ea**r
n	su**n**	eə	h**ai**r
ŋ	you**ng**	ʊə	**su**re
l	**l**ot	i	happ**y**
r	**r**un	uə	ann**u**al
j	**y**es		
w	**w**et		

ANSWER KEY

MODULE 0

1 a

2	woman	6	boy	10	student
3	teacher	7	desk	11	pen
4	chair	8	notebook	12	girl
5	door	9	window		

2

b	four	f	twenty
c	fifteen	g	three
d	two	h	twelve
e	eight		

3 a

2	Tuesday	5	Friday
3	Wednesday	6	Saturday
4	Thursday	7	Sunday

4

b thirty-five and fifty-four is eighty-nine
c twenty-nine and seventy-one is a hundred
d eighty-three and fourteen is ninety-seven

MODULE 1

1 a

2	's	5	name	8	And
3	What	6	Nice	9	this
4	your	7	you	10	Hello

2

b
1 's her name?
2 name's Nicole Kidman.
3 's she from?
4 's from Australia.

c
1 What are their names?
2 Their names are David and Victoria Beckham.
3 Where are they from?
4 They're from England.

d
1 What's his name?
2 His name's Jackie Chan.
3 Where's he from?
4 He's from China.

3

A	U	S	T	R	A	L	I	A	N
M	E	J	T	U	R	K	I	S	H
E	N	A	R	S	P	A	T	P	A
R	U	P	O	S	I	T	K	A	B
I	T	A	L	I	A	N	O	N	R
C	A	N	I	A	N	K	R	I	I
A	M	E	R	N	I	M	E	S	T
N	O	S	W	A	T	U	A	H	I
F	R	E	N	C	H	A	N	O	S
K	O	R	I	P	O	L	I	S	H
A	T	U	C	H	I	N	E	S	E

4

2	Brazilian	7	Egyptian
3	Swiss	8	Indonesian
4	Hungarian	9	Irish
5	Mexican	10	Argentinean
6	Canadian		

5

b	are	d	is	f	Are
c	Is	e	Are	g	is

6

b I'm not from Ireland.
c My mother and father aren't English.
d Brazil isn't a small country.
e My name isn't Lana.
f My sister isn't married.
g I'm not fifteen years old.
h Philip and Elizabeth aren't on holiday.

7

b	he is	g	he isn't
c	it isn't	h	they aren't
d	we aren't/we're not	i	it is
e	she is	j	she isn't
f	I am		

8

b	my	g	her
c	Her	h	his
d	our	i	our
e	our	j	your
f	their	k	My

9

b	a	f	a
c	an	g	a
d	a	h	an
e	a		

10

b	nurse	f	musician
c	police officer	g	lawyer
d	singer	h	electrician
e	shop assistant		

11 ^a

2	from	6	married
3	business	7	address
4	you	8	job
5	number		

12

b	Donna Fiorelli	f	Betty Booth
c	Béatrice Santini	g	David Mills
d	Plankton	h	Donna Fiorelli
e	David Mills		

13

b (My) mother's from the (United) (States).
c (Are) you (Spanish)?
d (Our) school is in (Camden) (Road).
e (I)'m from (Rome).
f (Eric) lives in (Berlin).

14 ^b

1   South London College
52 Richmond Road
London
SW15 6GS
UK

2   Mrs Mary Burke
109 St Stephen Street
Dublin
4
Ireland

c

Miss Sarah Ellis	Mr Simon Henderson
62 High Street	12 Muirfield
Amersham	Glasgow
HP7 6DJ	G12 8SJ
England	Scotland

15 ^b

2	/eɪ/	4	/ɒ/	6	/eɪ/	8	/ɒ/
3	/ɒ/	5	/aɪ/	7	/aɪ/		

MODULE 2

1

b	those	d	this	f	those
c	that	e	these		

2

b	an	d	an	f	–	h	an
c	a	e	–	g	a		

3

2	's got	5	've got	8	hasn't got
3	hasn't got	6	've got	9	's got
4	haven't got	7	's got		

4 ^a

2   Has she got a car?
Yes, she has.
3   Has she got a computer?
No, she hasn't.
4   Have Martin and Inge got a pet?
No, they haven't.
5   Have they got a car?
Yes, they have.
6   Have they got a computer?
Yes, they have.
7   Has Alfonso got a pet?
Yes, he has.
8   Has he got a car?
No, he hasn't.
9   Has he got a computer?
Yes, he has.

5 ^a

My friend Steve**'s** got a fantastic life. He**'s** only 21, but he**'s** got a great job – he**'s** a professional footballer – and he**'s** got lots of money. He**'s** got a new car, too – it**'s** a Porsche. It**'s** white and it**'s** got everything, even a CD player!

b

2	is	5	has	8	is
3	has	6	has	9	has
4	is	7	is		

6

b   Your dog has got **beautiful** eyes.
c   We've got two **black** cats at home.
d   I've got a **fantastic** computer game – Crash 5!!!
e   My friend Al is a **professional** musician.
f   Lauren Bacall is my **favourite** actress.
g   My sister's got a **new** mobile phone.
h   Goldie is a **friendly** dog.

7 ^a

2	a driving licence	8	an alarm clock
3	a lighter	9	an MP3 player
4	a lipstick	10	painkillers
5	a mirror	11	sun screen
6	a passport	12	toothpaste
7	a toothbrush		

8 ^a

2	son	5	parents	7	nephew
3	mother	6	husband	8	niece
4	father				

b
(Possible answers)
2   He's Joe and Brenda's son. He's Nora's grandson. He's Jane's brother. He's Sam's nephew.
3   He's Nora's son. He's Brenda's brother. He's Jane and Jason's uncle.

4   She's Joe's wife. She's Nora's daughter. She's Jane and Jason's mother. She's Sam's sister.
5   She's Joe and Brenda's daughter. She's Jason's sister. She's Nora's granddaughter. She's Colin's wife. She's Sam's niece.
6   They're Joe and Brenda's children. They're Nora's grandchildren. They're sister and brother.

9 b

1   Isabel Preyster
2   Chabeli
3   Julio Junior
4   Enrique

c
2   What are his children's names?
3   Are they all famous?
4   Who is Isabel Preysler?
5   What is Chabeli's job?
6   Is Julio Junior a singer?
7   Where is Enrique's home?
8   Has Enrique got a Porsche?

d
2   (Their names are) Chabeli, Julio Junior and Enrique.
3   Yes, they are.
4   She's their mother.
5   She's a journalist.
6   Yes, he is (and he's an actor and a model).
7   His home's in Miami, Florida.
8   Yes, he has. (He's got two!)

10

b   Is that Michael's car?
c   It's Tessa's birthday on Saturday.
d   What's your mother's name?
e   Where's Philip's desk?
f   My husband's name is Peter.
g   Jo is my sister's friend.
h   Carla's house is in the centre of Rome.

11 a

2   dictionaries   6   keys   10   buses
3   boxes   7   matches   11   addresses
4   universities   8   watches   12   boys
5   babies   9   houses

b
2   women   4   wives   6   people
3   businessmen   5   lives

12 a

What's this?
It's my passport.

b
His friend's name is James

c/d
1   This is my sister. Her name's Suzanne.
2   Those are my keys!
3   She's seven years old.
4   What's his address?
5   She's got fantastic blue eyes.
6   What's your brother's first name?
7   Sarah is a famous actress.
8   What's the answer to this question?

13

b   with   e   at   g   on
c   in   f   in   g   from
d   at

14

b   How   e   How   h   Who
c   Who   f   What   i   How
d   What   g   Where   j   What

15

b   My father's 42 and he's a lawyer.
c   My cousin Steve is 33 and he isn't married.
d   My parents have got a new car and it's fantastic..
e   Prague is the capital of the Czech Republic and it's very beautiful.
f   Maria and I are on holiday and we're in Thailand now.

MODULE 3

1

b   in a small house, with my family, in Mexico City
c   for Nike, long hours, in an office
d   to work, to university, to the cinema a lot
e   economics, law, at university
f   meat, a lot of fish, in restaurants a lot
g   coffee, black tea, mineral water

2 a

2   Do   7   of
3   out   8   study
4   drink   9   live
5   in   10   long
6   speak

3 a

2   Australia   4   to school   6   meat
3   Spanish   5   economics

4 b

2   live   10   don't live
3   speak   11   speak
4   don't speak 12   don't work
5   don't work 13   work
6   go   14   don't go
7   drink   15   don't drink
8   don't eat   16   eat

5

b   Yes, they do.   f   No, they don't.
c   No, they don't.   g   No, they don't.
d   No, they don't.   h   Yes, they do.
e   Yes, they do.

6 a

2   a school   6   a supermarket
3   a bank   7   a railway station
4   a hospital   8   a library
5   a hotel

7 b

2 They start at seven o'clock.
3 They have lunch at school.
4 They finish at six o'clock.
5 They go to the library.
6 They close at eleven or twelve o'clock.
7 They go home in a special minibus.
8 They go to bed at one or two o'clock.

8

b evening f a big meal
c get up g leave school
d close h the weekend
e come home

9

b It's half past three.
c It's five to seven.
d It's quarter past five.
e It's twenty past ten.
f It's quarter to four.
g It's twenty-five to twelve.
h It's five past nine.
i It's ten to one.

10

b on f in
c at g at
d in h in
e at

11

b the newspaper e shower h the bus
c bed late f TV i work
d dinner g home

12

b me e it g us
c it f it/me h them
d him

13 b

/ɪ/ six, big, finish, this, children, listen, dinner
/aɪ/ life, nine, five, write, night

14 a

In Britain children start school at about 9 o'clock in the morning, but in Poland they start school at 8 o'clock.

b

3 In New York most people start work at 8 a., but in York most people start work at 9 am.
4 In York most people start work at 9 a.m. and they finish work at 5.30 p.m.
5 In New York most people finish work at 6 pm, but in York they finish work at 5.30 pm.
6 In New York children start school at 5 years, but in York they start school at 4 years.
7 In New York most shops open at 9 am and they close at 8 pm.
8 In New York most shops close at 8 p.m., but in York they close at 6 pm.

15

b both e both g neither
c too f neither h too
d neither

MODULE 4

1

b watches e goes h studies
c comes f enjoys i plays
d lives g says

2 a

2 studies 4 speaks
3 lives 5 likes

c

2 He comes from Britain.
3 He lives in Seoul/South Korea.
4 He speaks English, French and Korean.
5 He plays the guitar.
7 She comes from Argentina.
8 She speaks Spanish, Catalan and English.
9 She works in a bank.
10 She goes to the gym.
12 He comes from Hungary.
13 He lives in Paris/France.
14 He teaches music.
15 He plays tennis.

3 a

3 No, she doesn't. 7 Yes, he does.
4 Yes, she does. 8 Yes, he does.
5 Yes, she does. 9 No, he doesn't.
6 No, he doesn't. 10 No, he doesn't.

4 a

2 It doesn't rain in summer.
3 My brother doesn't like getting up at seven o'clock.
4 The restaurant doesn't close on Sunday evening.
5 Martin doesn't come to class every week.
6 Tony doesn't buy all his food at the supermarket.
7 Carla doesn't drive to work.
8 My cousin doesn't visit me every month.

5

b leaves g drives l says
c writes h reads m doesn't work
d lives i buys n works
e gets up j sells
f has k finishes

6

b When does he get up?
c What does he do after breakfast?
d Where does he read the newspaper?
e Where does he go on holiday?
f What does he do after lunch?

7 ª

2	go for a run	7	go for a walk
3	wake up	8	meet friends
4	clean your teeth	9	get dressed
5	go to the gym	10	catch a bus
6	cook a meal		

8 ᵇ

2 Irene hates doing housework.
   Agnes loves doing housework.
3 Irene loves talking to the family.
   Agnes doesn't like talking to the family.
4 Irene likes going to English class.
   Agnes hates going to English class.
5 Irene doesn't like babysitting.
   Agnes likes babysitting.

9 ᵇ

2 In the south of France, or in Tuscany, in the north of Italy.
3 Paris.
4 London.
5 In a small house in Gascony.
6 In France.
7 Four.
8 The weather, the food and wine and the people.
9 England.

10

b	them	f	him
c	it	g	it
d	they	h	her/she
e	them		

11

b	sometimes	f	always
c	usually	g	never
d	never	h	always
e	often		

12

b	go/go	f	write/write
c	watch	g	visit
d	listen/listen	h	study
e	plays		

13

b Caroline **never** eats fish.
c I **don't** often eat in a restaurant.
d I **usually** get up late on a Sunday morning.
e It's **always** very hot in August in my city.
f The Brown family usually **go** to Italy on holiday.
g The weather is **always** cold in January.
h The bus is **often** late.

14 ᵇ

2	crowds	/z/	8	restaurants	/s/
3	spiders	/z/	9	houses	/ɪz/
4	actresses	/ɪz/	10	friends	/z/
5	beaches	/ɪz/	11	parents	/s/
6	drivers	/z/	12	addresses	/ɪz/
7	students	/s/			

15

b Excuse me, I'd like two coffees, please.
c I'd like one of those, please.
d Excuse me, I'd like the bill, please.
e Do you want milk with your tea?

16

b I'd like a coffee but I don't want milk, thank you.
c A: What's the time?
   B: I'm sorry, I haven't got a watch.
d A: Do you want a drink?
   B: That's a good idea!
e Is that Elena's bag?

17 ª

2	g	5	b	7	e
3	f	6	h	8	d
4	a				

b

My friend Takashi **comes from** Okinawa in Japan, but now he **lives** in London. **He's** a musician, and **he plays** in a bar called **East and West**. He likes the international atmosphere in London, but **he doesn't like** the rain. He **thinks** the people are very nice when you know them.

MODULE 5

1

b	motorbike	f	tram
c	scooter	g	train
d	bicycle	h	underground or subway
e	aeroplane	i	taxi

2

b	on	e	to	h	to/by
c	to	f	for	i	from
d	on	g	off/on	j	to

3

b	can	e	can't	h	can't
c	can't	f	can	i	can't
d	can't	g	can		

4 ª

2	Yes, you can.	5	Yes, you can.	7	No, it can't.
3	No, you can't.	6	Yes, you can.	8	Yes, you can.
4	No, they can't.				

5

c I always drive to work, but **a** lot of people come by underground.
d Parking is **a** real problem near my house.
e The traffic is very bad in **the** evening.
f My uncle is **a** train driver.
g Have you got **a** car?
h We live in **a** small town in **the** United States.

6

b Eight o'clock is a good time to phone Thomas: he is always at ~~the~~ home in the evening.
c It's so cold today that a lot of people can't go to ~~the~~ work.
d The train times are different on ~~the~~ Sundays.
e What do you think of the public transport in ~~the~~ London?
f You can use a Rail Card in most countries in ~~the~~ Europe.
g Do ~~the~~ people drive on the left in the United Arab Emirates?
h Our plane arrives in Los Angeles at ~~the~~ two o'clock in the afternoon.

7

b Not many people work on Sundays.
c A lot of British people go to Spain on holiday.
d Some people can't drink coffee without sugar.
e A lot of people don't like flying.
f Not many European people can understand Japanese.
g Most people in my town enjoy talking to tourists.
h Some people drive dangerously at night.

8 b

2 Moscow.
3 567.
4 The United States.
5 43,000,000.
6 Mexico City.
7 Grand Central Terminal Station, New York.
8 Six hours.

9

A
1 BA172 to Copenhagen. Here's my ticket.
2 No, only hand luggage.
3 Here's your boarding card. You're seat 25C.
4 Which gate is it?
5 Gate 14, but your flight's delayed by one hour.
B
6 That's £2.00.
7 When's the next train?
8 Which platform is it?
9 Platform 3.

10

b do   h Do
c Have   i is
d does   j does
e Is   k are
f Has   l can
g Can

11 b

/ɑː/	/eɪ/	/ɔː/	/æ/
can't	take	small	taxi
far	train	talk	traffic jam
car	wait	football	travel

12

2 hand luggage   8 a passenger
3 an overhead locker   9 a screen
4 a flight attendant   10 a seatbelt
5 a sign   11 the aisle
6 a window seat   12 an aisle seat
7 headphones

13

a Preston   f 737935C
b Robert   g AA9295
c 120283   h UK
d UK   i LIMA
e Male

MODULE 6

1 a

Fruit, meat, water, tea, cheese, music, bread, food, sugar

b
2 is   6 are
3 isn't/meals   7 These/are
4 takes   8 isn't
5 this/It's

2

Drinks: fruit juice, coffee, milk, tea
Types of fruit: apple, orange, grapes
Other things you can eat: cheese, ham, jam, yoghurt, eggs, toast, bread, butter, nuts, pizza, sausages, cereal

3

b	are there	f	there aren't
c	There's	g	There are
d	Are there	h	There isn't
e	Is there		

4 ᵃ

2 Are/Yes, there are.
3 Is/No, there isn't.
4 Is/Yes, there aren't.
5 Are/No, there isn't.
6 Are/Yes there are.

5 ᵃ

b	some	f	any
c	some/any	g	any/some
d	any	h	any/some
e	some		

6 ᵃ

2	no	6	any	10	some
3	a	7	no	11	a
4	some	8	some	12	a
5	An	9	A		

7 ᵃ

2	onions	7	carrots
3	peppers	8	peas
4	cabbages	9	potatoes
5	cucumbers	10	tomatoes
6	beans		

c

2	vinegar	6	herbs
3	French fries	7	crisps
4	oil	8	soy sauce
5	salad		

8

The correct picture is C.

9

b	How much	f	How much
c	How much	g	How many
d	How many	h	How many
e	How much		

10 ᵃ

2 Yes, can we have two steaks?
3 Would you like any vegetables?
4 Yes, some potatoes and peas, please.
5 Anything to drink with that?
6 We'd like a mineral water and a lemonade, please.

11 ᵃ

2	a bag	5	a glass
3	a packet	6	a bottle
4	a carton		

b

2	carton/bottle/glass	6	cup/packet
3	packet/bag	7	bottle/carton/glass
4	packet	8	cup/packet
5	bottle/glass		

12 ᵃ

2 You can <u>catch</u> a bus to the <u>airport</u> from here.
3 I <u>always</u> have <u>orange</u> juice with my <u>breakfast</u>.
4 <u>What</u> do you <u>want</u> for <u>lunch</u>?
5 I <u>never</u> drink <u>coffee</u> in the <u>evening</u>.

13 ᵃ

1	Italian	3	Argentinian
2	French	4	Hungarian

MODULE 7

1

b	was/was	f	weren't
c	were	g	was
d	were	h	was
e	were/wasn't		

2 ᵃ

3	Was/No, he wasn't.	7	Was/Yes, she was.
4	Was/Yes, he was.	8	Was/No, she wasn't.
5	Were/No, they weren't.	9	Were/No, they weren't.
6	Were/Yes, they were.	10	Were/Yes, they were.

3

b in two thousand and four
c from nineteen forty-six to nineteen fifty-five
d in the nineteen-fifties
e in the thirteenth century
f in nineteen ninety-eight
g from nineteen thirty-two to nineteen fifty-three
h in the eighteenth century

4

b	enjoyed	f	danced	j	tried
c	travelled	g	played	k	received
d	studied	h	believed	l	stayed
e	looked	i	arrived		

5

b	started/ended	e	helped	h	changed
c	died	f	studied	i	lived
d	walked	g	tried	j	worked

6

b	left	e	sang	h	won
c	went	f	sold	i	became
d	began	g	made		

7

b	from/to	f	on
c	at	g	In
d	in	h	in
e	At		

8ᵃ

3	S	6	S	9	S
4	D	7	S	10	D
5	D	8	S		

9ᵃ

2	flew	7	became	12	began
3	started	8	loved	13	received
4	arrived	9	tried	14	disappeared
5	wanted	10	gave	15	spent
6	met	11	left	16	found

10

b	fifth	f	twentieth
c	eighth	g	first/second
d	nineteenth	h	twenty-second
e	fourth		

11

b   January the thirtieth
c   November the seventeenth
d   August the twelfth
e   September the twenty-first
f   April the ninth

12

b   three years ago
c   when I was a child
d   when we were on holiday
e   every summer
f   yesterday evening
g   when they are eighteen
h   a week ago

13ᵃ

1	throw	5	cut	9	run
2	catch	6	fall	10	win
3	break	7	steal		
4	wake up	8	build		

b

2	catch	5	wake up	8	fall
3	build	6	run	9	cut
4	throw	7	steal	10	win

14ᵇ

A	3	C	4	E	2
B	1	D	5		

15

b	As a child	h	university
c	went to school	i	graduated
d	when I was	j	got a job
e	became interested	k	went to work
f	left	l	got married
g	studied		

16

b	After	e	Then	h	before
c	before	f	After		
d	Then	g	Before		

MODULE 8

1

b	comedy	f	horror film
c	action film	g	cartoon
d	musical	h	historical film
e	science fiction film		

2

E	N	J	O	Y	A	B	L	E	D	O
X	O	A	N	B	M	L	A	F	U	S
C	R	O	I	O	S	O	F	V	S	I
I	N	T	E	R	E	S	T	I	N	G
T	H	R	A	I	N	I	P	O	S	A
I	F	U	N	N	Y	L	O	L	T	R
N	Z	S	P	G	Q	L	B	E	C	G
G	K	A	M	R	U	Y	C	N	Y	H
M	A	D	R	O	M	A	N	T	I	C
E	X	A	P	W	H	O	Y	V	D	J
F	R	I	G	H	T	E	N	I	N	G

3

b	cost	g	found
c	gave	h	fell
d	drank	i	appeared
e	became	j	went
f	earned		

4

b   We didn't go for a drive yesterday.
c   Ben didn't remember to buy a birthday card.
d   I didn't hear the telephone.
e   The letter didn't arrive this morning.
f   I didn't eat in a restaurant last night.
g   Amanda didn't know what to do.
h   I didn't check my e-mail yesterday.

5

b   Did Alexander Graham Bell invent e-mail?
c   Did Marilyn Monroe sing 'Candle in the Wind'?
d   Did Captain Cook discover America?
e   Did Leonardo da Vinci paint 'Mona Lisa'?
f   Did Madonna play 'Evita'?
g   Did Beethoven write rock songs?
h   Did Laurel and Hardy make comedy films?
i   Did Yuri Gagarin travel to the moon?

6ᵃ

2	No, he didn't.	6	Yes, she did.
3	No, she didn't.	7	No, he didn't.
4	No, he didn't.	8	Yes, they did.
5	Yes, he did.	9	No, he didn't.

7 a

2 How did he
3 Where did he
4 How much did it
5 What did he buy
6 How many books did he
7 How much money did he
8 What time/When did he
9 How long did the journey

8

b Yes, I **did**.
c I didn't **buy** a newspaper yesterday.
d **Did** you listen to the news last night?
e No, I **didn't**.
f When I was 13, I always **wore** jeans.
g **Did** you use my computer this afternoon?
h I didn't **listen** to my parents when I was young.

9 b

/æ/   drank, ran, sang
/e/   read, fell, left, met
/ɔː/   caught, bought, saw, thought, wore
/ʌ/   cut, shut, won

10 a

2	front page	8	advertisement
3	headline	10	title
4	article	11	author
6	picture	12	cover
7	pages		

11 b

2 What did Atatürk do in 1915.
3 When did he become the first president of the Republic of Turkey.
4 When did he die?
5 When did Florence Nightingale work in a hospital for wounded soldiers?
6 What did the soldiers call her?
7 When did she begin a school of nursing in London?

12

b	haven't	f	was
c	let's	g	don't we
d	on	h	a
e	There's		

13 a

2	f	5	d	7	h
3	c	6	e	8	b
4	g				

b

3	sat	8	got	13	thought
4	helped	9	drove	14	remembered
5	spoke	10	saw	15	stopped
6	told	11	opened		
7	said	12	started		

MODULE 9

1

b	an easy question	e	a new bicycle
c	a small country	f	an uncomfortable chair
d	an ugly face	g	a fast train

2

b	easier	e	healthier	h	slimmer
c	bigger	f	newer	i	quieter
d	cheaper	g	happier	j	hotter

3 a

2 The River Mississippi is longer than the River Volga.
3 Blue whales are heavier than elephants.
4 The Pyramids in Egypt are older than the Parthenon in Greece.
5 The Sears Tower in Chicago is taller than the Eiffel Tower in Paris.
6 The Akashi-Kaikyo Bridge in Japan is longer than the Sydney Harbour Bridge in Australia.
7 Gold is more expensive than silver.
8 Esperanto is easier than English.

4 b

2 Karina Green is the youngest.
3 Karina Green has got the longest hair.
4 Jim Bowen has got the shortest hair.
5 Jim Bowen is the tallest.
6 Roy Seagrove is the heaviest.
7 Jake Kay is the smallest.
8 Roy Seagrove is the most successful.

5

b	smallest – Pluto	e	furthest/coldest – Pluto
c	biggest – Jupiter	f	easiest – Jupiter
d	hottest – Venus	g	closest – Venus

6 a

2	the biggest	6	most delicious
3	the best	7	bigger
4	larger	8	more expensive
5	bigger	9	better

7 c

1 Cats are bigger than tigers. ✗
2 Trains are faster than aeroplanes. ✗
3 Bicycles are slower than motorbikes. ✓
4 New York is older than Rome. ✗
5 Gold is more expensive than silver. ✓
6 Driving a car is more difficult than riding a bicycle. ✓

8

b	one is nearly three	d	one, please
c	the ones I bought	e	ones are the oldest

9

2	clothes shop	6	hairdresser
3	bakery	7	gift shop
4	post office	8	local store
5	pharmacy	9	dry cleaners

10

b The Ultimate Power Control System
c The Freezolux Smart Fridge
d The Bryson D838 Robot Vacuum Cleaner
e The Ultimate Power Control System
f The Bryson D838 Robot Vacuum Cleaner

11 a

2 it sells
3 The reason I like it is
4 is open
5 until eight o'clock at night
6 The best time to go is
7 The people there

12 a

1 customer
2 plastic bags
4 cashier
5 checkout
6 cans
7 shopping list
8 queue
9 shopping trolley
10 shopping basket

13

1
B: Yes, in the Food Hall.
A: Which floor is that?
B: It's on the ground floor.

2
A: Have you got these shoes in a size 38?
B: What colour would you like?
A: Black or brown.

3
A: Can I buy these, please?
B: That's £49.99.
A: Do you take credit cards?
B: Yes, visa or mastercard?

4
A: Can I have one of those, please?
B: One of these?
A: Yes. How much is it?
B: It's 75p.

5
A: What time does the supermarket close?
B: We are open all night.

14

a Julia's
b Your/mine
c Gardener's/her
d theirs
e Our
f his
g Its
h Monroe's/hers
i ours
j Tony's/mine

MODULE 10

1

b studying
c washing
d leaving
e coming
f stopping
g making
h dancing
i staying
j giving
k planning
l writing

2 a

2 is looking
3 is talking
4 is sitting
5 is eating
6 is having
7 is watching
8 are doing

3 a

2 Where/d
3 Why/a
4 Who/b
5 What/c
6 What/e

4

b No, it isn't.
c Yes, they are.
d Yes, we are.
e No, I'm not.
f Yes, he is.
g No, she isn't.

5 a

2 Are you enjoying
3 I'm not
4 I'm not having
5 's happening
6 They're playing
7 's dancing
8 Is she dancing
9 she isn't
10 She isn't doing
11 She's looking
12 isn't listening
13 's he doing
14 's coming

6

b do you come
c Do you speak
d It's raining
e I'm watching
f drive
g are you doing/I'm waiting
h Are you reading
i We're having

7

b Marie
c Marie
d Paul
e Paul
f Marie
g Paul
h Bob
i Paul
j Paul
k Bob
l Bob

8

b 5
c 10
d 3
e 1
f 9
g 4
h 6
i 11
j 13
k 8
l 2
m 12

9

	Where is she from?	What clothes does she talk about?	Where did she buy her clothes?
Mina	London	jeans, jumper, jacket, shoes	Michiko, *Space*, Camden Market
Gloria	Barcelona, Spain	dress, trousers, shoes	She made them herself – she bought her shoes in Spain but she can't remember where from.
Alice	United States	top, trousers, shoes, jacket	Milan, New York

10 a

2 Everybody says she**'s** very good-looking.
3 Where**'s** Frank going?
4 Who**'s** the girl with long dark hair?
5 Dina**'s** got short hair.
6 David**'s** mother doesn't wear glasses.
7 Ann**'s** the black girl with medium-length hair.
8 Maria**'s** waiting for me in the car.

b

2 = is   3 = is   4 = is   5 = has   6 = possessive   7 = is
8 = is

11 a

b Excuse me, have you got **the** time please?
c Is this bus going **to** the city centre?
d Is **it** okay to park here?
e Is **this** the way to the station?
f What time **do** the shops close on Saturdays?

b

1	b	3	f	5	e
2	d	4	a	6	c

12

b	sitting	f	he's	j	she's
c	shining	g	has	k	look
d	are	h	isn't	l	attractive
e	wearing	i	eyes		

MODULE 11

1 b

3 She can't
4 She can
5 can speak French
6 can play chess
7 He can't drive a car.
8 He can't play a musical instrument.

2 a

2 Can she play chess?
   No, she can't.
3 Can she drive a car?
   Yes, she can.
4 Can she play a musical instrument?
   Yes, she can.
5 Can Max speak French?
   No, he can't.
6 Can he play chess?
   Yes, he can.
7 Can he drive a car?
   Yes, he can.
8 Can he play a musical instrument?
   No, he can't.

3

b	What kind	e	How long	h	What
c	When	f	What colour	i	How
d	Which	g	What time	j	How well

4 b

2 How fast can they run?
3 How many humps does a dromedary have?
4 How many camels are there in the world?
5 How tall is an adult camel?
6 How much does an adult camel weigh?
7 How far can camels walk without drinking?
8 How often do camels need to drink water?
9 How much water can they drink?

5

b	How many	e	Which	h	How much
c	Which	f	How much	i	What
d	How much	g	How many		

6

b How many films did he make?
c How long does a football match last?
d Where was the boxer Muhammad Ali born?
e How far is your home from here?
f What kind of music do you like?
g How fast can a cheetah run?
h What is the biggest ocean in the world?

7

b	did	f	did
c	do	g	can
d	is	h	was
e	were		

8 a

1	horse	5	cow	9	frog
2	dog	6	bee	10	mouse
3	sheep	7	monkey	11	beetle
4	duck	8	spider	12	snake

c

Animals with two legs   duck, monkey
Animals with four legs   frog, cow, mouse, sheep, horse, dog
Animals with more than four legs   bee, beetle, spider

9

b up to 6 metres
c 6 cm
d about 3 kg
e more than 2.5 metres
f 20 to 50 times a second
g more than 50
h i) 13 million   ii) a few hundred   iii) about 50,000

10 a

2	1985	7	62,000,000
3	3,000	8	297
4	90 km/h	9	2,000,000,000
5	9.6	10	963
6	253,000		

b

2 one hundred and fifty kilometres an hour
3 three million
4 eight point five
5 three hundred and forty-eight
6 two billion
7 five thousand six hundred
8 nineteen eighty
9 three hundred and fifty thousand
10 eighty million

12

b	—	f	the/the	j	the
c	the	g	—	k	the
d	a	h	the	l	the
e	a	i	an		

13

b I'm not sure what the answer **is.**
c Is it true that koala bears don't drink water**?**
d What is the world's largest animal**?**
e He doesn't know the answer**.**
f Where's the biggest lake in the world**?**
g What is Peter's pet dog's name**?**

MODULE 12

1 ^a

2 He's going to buy a newspaper.
3 They're going to play tennis.
4 The bus is going to stop.
5 They're going to get wet.
6 He's going to go to bed.
7 They're going to paint the ceiling.
8 They're going to have lunch.

2

b	I don't want to	f	She wants to
c	She doesn't want to	g	He doesn't want to
d	Does anybody want to	h	Do you want
e	Do your friends want to		

3

b	No, he isn't.	f	No, they don't.
c	Yes, they do.	g	Yes, she is.
d	No, she doesn't.	h	Yes, he does.
e	Yes, he is.	i	Yes, they are.

4 ^a

2 Would you like something to drink?
3 My friends and I would like a table near the window, please.
4 Marc doesn't want to stay at home.
5 Which film would you like to see this evening?
6 I'd like to order a taxi, please.
7 We don't want any more coffee, thank you.
8 Would you like to go for a walk in the park?

5

b Tomorrow's Saturday ... I'**m** going to stay in bed all day.
c Where do you want **to** go?
d Would you **like** to go out for lunch?
e Chris isn't enjoying his holiday: he **wants** to go home!!
f My friends are going **to** cook a special meal this evening.
g What would you like **to** do tomorrow?
h We **are** not going to have a holiday this year.

6

a a meal, a shower
b in bed, at home
c television, a video
d the shopping, your homework, the housework
e the gym, the country, the cinema, a concert
  (you can also go to a party and a barbecue)

7 ^a

2	don't want	5	about	8	like
3	Let's	6	there's	9	idea
4	see	7	don't	10	I'll

9

b	to	e	in	h	on
c	at	f	at		
d	in	g	to		

10 ^a

1	the sky	7	a surfer
3	a cloud	8	a beach umbrella
4	waves	10	a towel
5	a windsurfer	11	a sandcastle
6	rocks	12	the beach

11 ^a

tonight
tomorrow morning
tomorrow evening
this weekend
next week
next month
next year

b

2	tomorrow evening	5	next month
3	next week	6	next year
4	this weekend	7	this evening/tonight

12

Chicago	snow, windy	–
San Francisco	heavy rain	–
Queensland	heavy rain	475 mm of rain in five days
Jerez de la Frontera	hot, sunny	30 degrees – warmest so far
	this year	
The Balkans	heavy snow	–
North-east Italy	heavy snow	on Monday and Tuesday
Irkutsk	above zero	first time since last November

13

b It's sunny.   e It's warm.   h It's cold.
c It's hot.   f It's cloudy.   i It's windy.
d It's foggy.   g It's snowing.

14

2 b   3 a   4 f   5 c   6 e

MODULE 13

1

B	Geography	H	Mathematics
C	Information Technology	I	Engineering
D	History	J	Law
E	Literature	K	Design
F	Medicine	L	Politics
G	Science	M	Economics

2

b secondary   g pass
c get   h failed
d for   i getting
e do   j choose
f take

3

b She went to the library to borrow some books.
c She went to the post office to send a parcel to her cousin.
d She went to the hospital to visit her sick friend.
e She went to the greengrocer's to buy some fruit.
f She went to the butcher's to buy some meat.
g She went to the bus station to catch the bus.
h She went to the Oak Tree Café to have lunch.

4

b to get   d to buy   f to watch
c be   e pass   g have

5

B 5   C 1   D 4   E 2

6

2 desk   5 keyboard   8 mouse
3 document   6 screen   9 modem
4 printer   7 CD-ROM drive   10 scanner

7

2 The plane might arrive late.
3 You might be rich one day, if you work hard.
4 I might not be able to come to class next week.
5 I might not see Frank this weekend.
6 Philip might not stay until the end of the course.
7 The government might change soon.
8 The exam might not be as difficult as you think.

8 a

2 There probably won't be time to stop for lunch.
3 Martha will probably be late for class.
4 You probably won't need your umbrella.
5 I probably won't be able to come tomorrow.
6 There will probably be an election soon.

9 b

2 Meg will probably go to Spain with her parents.
3 Sampath probably won't have time for a holiday.
4 Tom might not go to university.
5 Meg will probably go to university next year.
6 Sampath might get a job abroad instead.
7 Tom will probably work for his father's company.
8 Meg will probably become a doctor.
9 Sampath might become an actor.

12 a

2 Jan   6 Dec
3 Oct   7 No
4 Dr   8 Sep
5 n/a   9 etc.

b

2 exempli gratia (= for example)
3 kilograms
4 kilometres
5 Monday, Tuesday, Wednesday, Thursday
6 North, South, East, West
7 Park
8 Road
9 Street
10 telephone
11 United Kingdom
12 United States of America

c

2 2 kg
3 63 Stamford St
4 irregular verbs, e.g. bring and buy
5 Queen's Pk Rd
6 London SW7
7 10 km
8 arrived in the UK from the USA
9 tel no: 020 7939 3671
10 classes are on Tues and Thurs
11 Jan–Mar and Apr–Sep

MODULE 14

1

b writing a letter   g making a telephone call
c sending an e-mail   h sending a card
d sending a fax   i sending something by post
e taking a photo   j receiving a text message
f surfing the Internet   k paying by phone

2 a

1 slept   5 spoken   9 said   13 told
2 made   6 taken   10 come   14 become
3 lost   7 driven   11 given   15 seen
4 stoo   8 written   12 kept
mystery word: past participles

3

b	have seen	g	have forgotten
c	have left	h	have checked
d	has written	i	have bought
e	has lost	j	has never had
f	have never read		

4 b

2	has won	7	have played
3	haven't had	8	hasn't won
4	has played	9	has scored
5	has never lost	10	has been
6	has been		

5 a

2	Has/Yes, she has.	6	Have/No, they haven't.
3	Have/No, they haven't.	7	Has/No, she hasn't.
4	Has/No, he hasn't.	8	Has/Yes, she has.
5	Has/Yes, he has.		

6 a

2	gone	4	got
3	fed	5	shown

7

b	✓	e	✗ studied	h	✗ played
c	✗ tried	f	✓	i	✗ lived
d	✓	g	✓	j	✗ travelled

8

b	ever	e	never
c	recently	f	always
d	already	g	just

9

b They've just got married.
c We've (recently) bought a flat in Dubai (recently).
d My father's never been on a tram before.
e Stefanie's already studied the present perfect.
f Have you ever slept outside?

10 a

b haven't seen
c spoke
d Have you ever been
e went
f Did you like
g was
h Have you ever sold
i haven't
j tried
k bought
l 've already paid.

11

b I'm sorry, he's not **here** at the moment.
c Can you ask him **to** phone me, please?
d What's your number?
e Hello, SA International, **can** I help you?
f I'**d** like to speak to Mr Cornwell, please.
g I'**ll** connect you.
h Is **that** Jim Cornwell?
i Hello, **this** is Susan Heyman from Business Solutions.
j Oh hi, Susan. How **are** you?
k **this** is Matthew speaking.
l Please leave **a** message after the tone.

12 a

2	postman	7	post box
3	note	8	parcel
4	envelope	9	stamps
5	postcard	10	posting a letter
6	birthday card		

13 a

2 Fiona
3 to the supermarket
4 6 o'clock

b

Thanks for feeding cats.
Tins of cat food in cupboard next to window.
Please give one tin ONLY!!
See you on Saturday, about 1.
Love
Tom

MODULE 15

1

b the art gallery
c the sports stadium
d the shopping centre
e the museum
f the beach
g the park
h the canal
i the mosque
j the palace

2

bridge, castle, directions, end, fantastic, gallery, hill, interesting, journey, kilometre, mountain, necessary, open, park, river, statue, ticket, under, walk

3

b	over	f	across
c	up	g	from
d	to	h	into
e	past		

4

b from
c over
d out of
e down

f across
g along
h past

5

b doesn't have to
c has to
d has to
e doesn't have to

f has to
g don't have to
h don't have to

6 ^a

2 Does he have to use a computer?
No, he doesn't.
3 Does he have to look smart?
Yes, he does.
4 Does George have to fly the plane?
Yes, he does.
5 Does he have to serve food?
No, he doesn't.
6 Does he have to wear a uniform?
Yes, he does.
7 Do Alizia and Meera have to wear a uniform?
No, they don't.
8 Do they have to travel a lot?
No, they don't.

7 ^a

2 can
3 don't have to
4 can
5 have to

6 can
7 have to
8 can't
9 have to

10 can't
11 can
12 can't

8

	Blue Lagoon	London Bridge	Guggenheim Museums
What it is	a beach	a bridge and shopping/ watersports centre	museum/ collection of modern art
Where it is	45 km from Reykjavik, Iceland	Lake Havasu City, Arizona, USA	New York, Italy, Berlin, Bilbao, on the Internet
Why people go there	to swim	to see the bridge and see the English village, shops and restaurants	to see paintings and other works of art

9 ^a

2 straight
3 turn
4 on

5 past
6 the
7 on

c
2 turn
3 Take
4 on
5 go
6 past

7 When
8 left
9 on
10 right

10 ^a

2 a department store
3 a clothes shop
4 a bench
5 a pushchair
6 automatic doors

7 shoppers
8 steps
9 an escalator
10 a shop window

11

b fashionable
c attractive
d lively
e traditional
f peaceful
g interesting
h expensive
i friendly
j modern

12 ^a

2 straight
3 scenery
4 highest
5 building

6 through
7 design
8 know
9 sights

10 right
11 sign
12 listen

13 ^a

2 in
3 great
4 seen

5 tea
6 nearest
7 have

8 English
9 Bye

Pearson Education Limited
Edinburgh Gate
Harlow
Essex CM20 2JE
England
and Associated Companies throughout the world.

www.longman.com/cuttingedge

First published 2005

ISBN 0 582 825032

Set in ITC Stone Informal and Congress Sans

Printed by Mateu Cromo, S.A. Pinto, Spain

Designed by Cathy May (Endangered Species)

Project Managed by Lindsay White

Author Acknowledgements
The publisher and author would like to thank the following people for their help and
contribution:
Sarah Cunningham and Peter Moor for their support and encouragement and every-
one at Pearson who has contributed to the project: Jonathan Barnard; Rachel Bladon;
Jenny Colley; Sally Cooke; Sue Donoghue; Alma Gray; Tina Gulyas; Cathy May;
Sarah Munday; Ann Oakley; Shona Rodger; Lindsay White.

Photo Acknowledgements
We are grateful to the following for permission to reproduce copyright photographs:
Alamy for page 25; Art Directors and TRIP for 8 bottom left; Corbis for 21 (all), 39 bot-
tom left, 41 middle, 91 middle; Getty One Stone for 64 top, 64 bottom right, 67 top
right, 67 middle right; Hulton Getty for 41 top, 50 bottom; Getty Images for 50 top;
Image Bank for 8 top left; Empics for 40; Frank Lane Picture Agency for 64 bottom
left, 67 top left, 67 middle left, 67 bottom; Jeff Moore for 8 bottom right; Pearson
Education for 49 left (Trevor Clifford) and 49 middle (Peter Lake); Peter Newark's
American Pictures for 41 bottom; PA Photos for 5 middle, 5 bottom right; The
Photographers Library for 49 right; Popperfoto for 13, 39 top right, 39 bottom right,
83, 91 top; Powerstock Zefa for 18; Rex Features for 5 top; Frank Spooner Pictures for
39 middle, 91 bottom; Sporting Pictures for 5 bottom left; Woodfin Camp for 8 top
right.

Picture research by Sue Donoghue

Illustrated by Jeff Anderson, Gary Andrews, Kes Hankin (Gemini Design), Connie
Jude, Chris Pavely, Theresa Tibbetts (Beehive Illustration Agency), Mark Vallance
(Gemini Design).

Cover photo © Getty Images/Image Bank.